ENDORSEMENTS

" . . . *children are being taught to value imagination by learning through literature rather than formulaic text. Now* **Raspberry Publications** *offers a special incentive—publication—to make books an even more exciting part of their lives.*"

Emily McCully
Children's Book Author and Illustrator
Recipient of the 1993 Caldecott Medal
New York, New York

"*I commend* **Raspberry Publications** *for acknowledging and rewarding the creative work of children. By recognizing the written endeavors of children,* **Raspberry Publications** *provides an opportunity for success that leads to an incentive for future accomplishments. I am extending my endorsement for Ariel Gonzalez's award winning work,* **The Magic Pencil**. *This bright, young fourth grader has written a book that is to be respected and admired by all ages. By combining talent and imagination, Ariel is able to touch our lives and stimulate our desire for fantasy*".

Congressman Gene Green
House of Representatives
Washington, DC

"*I believe that books written by children for children can play an important role in increasing a child's self-esteem and communications plus the added confidence these skills will generate can help children develop into productive adults.*"

Congressman John Kasich
House of Representatives
Washington, DC

"**Raspberry Publications** *encompasses so many of the instructional techniques that we advocate . . . it enforces and enhances communication and thinking skills . . . and it allows children to speak, in important ways, to each other.*"

Paula Cummins, Director
Summer Laureate University for Youth
University of Arkansas

"*An authentic tale,* **A Monster In My Mouth**, *amusingly and honestly recounts a common childhood experience.*"

Kathy Shahbodaghi
Children's Librarian
Columbus, Ohio

"Kaitlin's books are a joy. **The Cat Sat** *should be right next to* The Cat in the Hat *on every beginning reader's bookshelf and* **A Monster In My Mouth** *should be in every orthodontist's office."*
> Melinda McDonald
> Sheridan Junior High School
> Sheridan, Arkansas

"The Whale Dancers *is a wonderful story. I only hope that Anne E. Kafoure continues to use her talents for storytelling and illustrating on behalf of the animal world. Her portrayal of the wild whales is accurate and sensitive, and her understanding of the feelings and conflict felt by Toyo are real and heartfelt. Anne has a special gift, and I am pleased to recommend this book not only to animal lovers, but to anyone looking for a unique story about feelings and making choices."*
> Jack Hanna
> Director Emeritus, Columbus Zoo
> Columbus, Ohio

"Anne E. Kafoure has written words that will touch the minds and hearts of every age reader. Although she resides in a moderate sized suburban community and has not yet graduated from public school, she belongs to the world. The recognition Anne receives from this distinguished literary and artistic effort will not only contribute to her sense of accomplishment and selfworth, but will serve as a "real world in the classroom" connection for everyone around her."
> Ernest A. Husarik, Ph.D.
> Superintendent, Westerville City Schools
> 1993 Top 100 Educators in North America
> (Executive Director)
> 1994 Ohio Superintendent of the Year
> Westerville, Ohio

"The Magic Pencil *is a wonderful tale that shows not only Ariel's writing talents, creativity and imagination, but also his strong sense that encouraged him to use newly found powers to assist others in times of need."*
> Dr. Rod Paige, Superintendent
> Houston Independent School District
> Houston, Texas

"The Magic Pencil *exemplifies the role education plays in the development of children and youth. This young author has opened new worlds for both himself and his readers by stretching his young and fertile imagination and using the most valuable resource the world of the future has . . . the minds of it's children."*
> Herlinda Garcia, Principal
> Henderson Elementary School
> Houston, Texas

To Miss Hill's class —

Young Author's Guide to Publishers

Third Edition

Tracey E. Dils

Tracey E. Dils

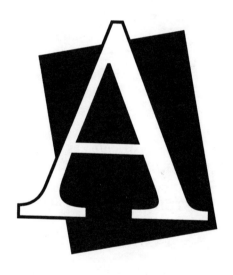

RASPBERRY PUBLICATIONS, INC., WESTERVILLE, OHIO

PUBLISHERS

Curtis E. Jenkins   Susan B. Schmidt

Graphic Design
by
Driftwood Media

Distributed by

RASPBERRY PUBLICATIONS, INC.
P.O. BOX 925
WESTERVILLE, OH 43086-6925
1-800-759-7171
FAX: (614) 899-6147

ISBN: 1-884825-20-6

PRINTED AND BOUND IN THE
UNITED STATES OF AMERICA

THIRD EDITION

Dedication

To Sara Jean Wilhelm, who taught me to believe in myself as a writer.

With thanks to Lillian, Emily, Alison, Lizzy, Hillary, Sarah, Katherine, and Michelle, the members of the Barrington Elementary After School Writing Program.

And a special thank you to Jen Thackeray, Gwen Kerr, and my children, Emily and Phillip.

Tracey

TABLE OF CONTENTS

FOREWORD

We are honored to have Ms. Tracey E. Dils, a distinguished author of children's books, as the featured author of this year's Young Author's Guide to Publishers.

Ms. Dils has created a valuable resource for all young authors and we hope you enjoy her style and experienced instructions on what it takes to become a published author.

The editors at Raspberry would also like to hear from you. Tell us what you would like to see in our upcoming editions. What you like and don't like so we can make our book better for you to use.

ACKNOWLEDGEMENTS

We would like to express our appreciation to all the editors and publishers who graciously responded to our requests for updated information because we know how precious their time is.

Our special thanks to Laura Hembree and Jennifer Bosveld for their contributions on playwriting and poetry. They add a special dimension to our new edition.

A special thanks to all the librarians, teachers and children who pointed out our mistakes and continued to support us with their hearts and skills. We thank them for their criticisms and we promise to make all our new publications even better and as free of mistakes as we possibly can.

This edition is for all of you who have never lost faith in our children.

Thank you.

LETTER FROM THE PUBLISHERS

When we created Raspberry Publications as a publisher of young people's work we knew there were lots of talented writers out there. We just didn't know how many! The world of children's literature has always been dominated by adult artists and authors. Many of them are exceptional storytellers and have given us everlasting works of art. But in the beauty and wonderment of these talented creations, we have over-looked the readers of these books; the children themselves.

Why are more young authors not published? Is it because children's works are not good enough? We don't think so because we have seen and published some exceptional works created entirely by children. Perhaps some adults think that what young people have to say isn't worthwhile; we hope not because that means they are saying our children have no value. We at Raspberry believe all our children have value and deserve more opportunities to become published authors.

In our many visits to schools, we are always pleasantly surprised by the universal acceptance we receive from the teachers, librarians and others in the educational community. They tell us how their students love to read what other children have written and that they are motivated by seeing books created by their peers. Their outstanding encouragement and dedication to our children is without equal and we are grateful-ly indebted to all of them. We are proud to know all of them and to offer another publishing opportunity for their students' work.

The road to becoming a published author is an exciting and simple one, as long as you have infinite patience, a strong will to succeed, a determined desire to get into print and plenty of persistence.

Works by people like you are put into print every day. They started with the same blank page, suffered the same doubts and lived through the same rejections before it hap-pened, but they never stopped and neither should you.

Curt Jenkins   Susan Schmidt

A LETTER FROM THE AUTHOR

Dear Writer,

When I visit schools to talk about my writing, I am frequently asked, "When did you become a writer?"

It's not an easy question to answer. I have been writing for young readers for about ten years and have written twelve books for children. Before that, I was a book editor. Before that, I wrote encyclopedia articles for a living. And during high school and college, I wrote for literary magazines and newspapers.

But I considered myself a writer before all that happened. In fact, I've called myself a writer for so long that I sometimes can't remember when I *became* one.

As early as third grade, I remember writing a poem called "The Dance of the Snowmen." My mother copied and included it in her Christmas cards. In fourth grade, writing meant practicing penmanship. While my friends used cartridge pens to copy over poems written by famous writers in flowing script, I wrote my own poems. I remember one of them called "A Book Is a Dream" about books and the many places they could take readers. My teacher wasn't very happy that I wasn't doing the work she asked me to do, but she knew that I was following my dream, a very special dream.

What did that dream of writing mean to me? It meant I could make myself heard. It meant that I could make people laugh, cry, or dream their own dreams. It meant I could take my readers to places that they had *never* dreamed of.

It also meant that I was different. Because I felt my writing made me different, I carried my dream inside me like some delicious secret. I shared it with only a few friends and teachers, those whom I thought would understand. And then I realized that, even if no one else understood my dream, I understood it. Writing made me different, all right, but it also made me special. That's when I developed the courage to share it with others. That's when I really *became* a writer.

Today, the world is a wonderful place for writers. Schools

teach poetry instead of penmanship. Writers keep journals and share their writing with friends and teachers. Teachers and parents love to hear the stories from young writers. And some publishing companies—like Raspberry Publications and others mentioned in this book—publish the work of young writer' like you.

If you are a writer, you know that your ability to write is what makes you special. That's not a secret that you need to keep. Let your school know, your teachers know, your parents know that you *are* a writer.

And let me know about you, too. I want to hear about your dreams, your successes, your special writing problems. Please write to me in care of Raspberry Publications. We'll share just how special writing makes both of us feel.

But just now I want to share my dream for you. My dream is that you become a writer and that this book is one of the tools that shows you the way. My dream for you is that this book helps you to become the best writer you can be.

Sincerely,

Tracey E. Dils

CHAPTER ONE

TAKING YOURSELF SERIOUSLY AS A WRITER

Since you are holding this book in your hands, you probably enjoy writing. Whether in the classroom at school, at writer's workshops in your community, or alone in your room, you probably like to invent stories, pen poems, write long letters to friends, or create your own plays. You may carry a journal with you wherever you go and jot down little musings. You may actually switch off the television to work on your latest creation. You probably share what you've written with friends, maybe even publishing your own little books.

But are you a writer?

A writer is different from someone who writes. A writer takes the job of writing very seriously. A writer seeks the opinions of others and takes their criticism seriously. A writer revises manuscripts many, many times and, even then, is never quite satisfied with his or her work, sometimes even when it's in print.

And many serious writers seek to publish their work in magazines, newspapers, or in book form. And that's where this book can be a big help.

How do you know if you are a serious writer? What does it mean to take yourself seriously as a writer? How do you know if you have what it takes to be published?

I AM A WRITER

Let's start with the basic way that you see yourself. When someone asks you who you are, you probably tell them your name and your age or grade. If someone asks you what you like to do, you might say that you like to write or that you want to be a writer some day or that you dabble in poetry or write a few stories in your spare time.

Try saying this instead: *I AM A WRITER.*

Serious writers identify themselves as writers first and foremost. Even if you are young and are trying out lots of different activities, if you want to be a writer, it's important to start identifying yourself as a writer in the "list" of ways that you talk about yourself.

Next time someone asks you about yourself, try this:
I am Emily Herrold, I am in fourth grade, I like to play soccer, and I am a writer.

That feels a lot different than saying, *I want to be a writer, someday* or *I like to write,* doesn't it?

SERIOUS WRITERS ARE SERIOUS READERS

If you are like most writers, you probably read almost as much as you write. You probably like to read for fun and you may read to learn more about the writing process. That's important—reading a wide variety of books is one way that serious writers find their own voice and develop their own style.

How do you make the most of your reading habit? What's the best way to learn from what other writers have done?

One way is to read a wide range of material. That may mean selecting some things to read that you wouldn't normally pick out just for pleasure. If you are already reading chapter books or novels for fun, try and read some nonfiction or information books for a change. If you like to read nonfiction stories in kid's magazines, check out some of the articles in your local newspaper or ask your parents if they can show you some articles of interest in the magazines that they read. If you like to read poems by modern-day poets like Jack Prelutsky or Shel Silverstein, take some time to read the classics. Ask your grandparents or parents what some of their favorites are and read them together. Check out or buy an anthology of the *world's best-loved poems* and work your way through it, getting a sense of what writers have written throughout history.

But it's not enough to just read a wide range of material. You'll also want to take time to jot down notes about what you read and to really study how other writers have developed their craft. Here are some simple ways to do that:

When was the last time that you were deeply moved by something that you've read? Have you ever cried while you were reading a novel? Has something you read made you so mad that you were ready to burst? Have you ever laughed out loud as you were reading?

Take note of these emotions. Go back and see what the author did to make you feel the way that you did. Perhaps it was the character who made you cry, as Beth did when she died in *Little Women*. Perhaps it was the way that the author used specific detail about homeless people, for instance, that made you so mad. Maybe it was a silly pun or a bizarre plot twist that made you laugh out loud. Keep a journal where you record the techniques that some of your favorite authors have used. Then, when you want to pull a deep emotion from a reader, look back at your notes and see if you can use some of the same techniques these experts used.

Another way to take advantage of your reading habit, especially if you are reading fiction, is to make notes about story structure. You may even want to make a story map, web, or outline that plots out the action in one of your favorite novels or short stories. Think about these elements: What are the key events in the plot? When is the conflict introduced? What steps does the main character take to deal with that conflict? How many scene changes are there per chapter? How many episodes per chapter? How do the chapters end and begin? How often does the author use dialogue to move the plot along? Are there cliffhangers that make you want to keep reading? What is it about the book that makes you unable to put it down?

At the same time that you are making notes about what has worked in a piece of writing, you'll also want to take note of what *hasn't* worked. What don't you like about a particular story or novel? Is there any part of the story that you don't

believe or that doesn't seem real to you? Do the characters seem
to react like real kids in the same situation would react? Do the
kid-characters seem in charge of solving the story's problem?
Do you feel empathy for the story's main character?

SERIOUS WRITERS WRITE AS MUCH AS THEY CAN

Serious writers write as much as they can—every day, if
possible. Many serious writers make writing as much a part of
their daily routine as a morning walk or brushing their teeth.
Even if they aren't working on a project, they spend some time
each day just working on their craft—developing characters,
sketching out plots, or crafting a few lines of a poem.

If you have a busy schedule of school work and other
activities, you may have to consciously make time for your
writing. Pick a time of day when you are likely to be alone—
perhaps early in the morning, during a lunch break, or just
after dinner in the evening. Then try to reserve that time for
writing. You may want to try and write for at least half an hour
at a single sitting. Or you may find it easier to set a goal for how
much you want to write, instead of how long. You might try and
write three pages a day, for instance, or 750 words.

Of course, serious writers also master the art of "writing on
the fly," writing when they are suddenly inspired by an idea.
Always carry a note pad or a journal with you wherever you go,
even if you just use it to jot down a few thoughts or ideas that
may work themselves into a poem or an article later on. You
may even want to carry a small hand-held tape recorder with
you to record your thoughts if you are in the car, on the bus, or
taking a long walk.

SERIOUS WRITERS REVISE

Perhaps the biggest thing that separates serious writers
from those who write is the fact that serious writers revise. In
fact, most serious writers spend as much time—or more time—
revising their work as they do writing it the first time.

Chapter Two will give you some guidelines for revising your

work. Just remember, good writing takes time and serious writers take time with their work. (I have spent up to four years revising a short picture book—and, even though it's been published, I still see a few things that I would have done differently if I had another chance.)

PUBLISHING IS FOR SERIOUS WRITERS ONLY

There are many reasons to write—and, if you are a serious writer, you probably have very personal reasons of your own for wanting to put your thoughts down on paper. If publishing is one of your writing goals, though, you need to recognize that the publishing world is a competitive place. It's tough to get an editor at a publishing house to look at your manuscript, let alone publish it. And it's even tougher to be published as a young writer, because many publishing houses simply don't consider the work of young writers. That's why you need to be serious about the business of writing and submitting your work.

This book shows you how to do just that. In Chapter Four, you'll find tips on researching appropriate publishers, preparing and packaging your manuscript, writing a cover letter to an editor, and following up. The best way to get these tips to work for you, though, is to begin thinking of yourself as a serious writer and treating what you do as professionally as you can.

Remember you *are* a writer and the work you do is important. The more seriously you take it, the more seriously the publishing world will take your work.

TIPS FOR SERIOUS YOUNG AUTHORS

• Think of yourself as a writer. Say, *I am a writer*, instead of *I want to be a writer someday.*

• Set up a writing place, a place that is all yours where you can really devote yourself to writing. It may be as small as a corner of your own room or a hillside at the park. Call this place your writing place and visit it every day—or as often as you can.

• Start or join a writer's group. Try forming a writer's group with your fellow writers. Share feedback, writing tips, and successes.

• Revise. A writer is never satisfied with his work. Spend time revising, even if you are tired of what you've written.

• Enter every contest that you can. Many local papers sponsor contests for young writers. Find out about them.

• Develop a daily writing habit.

• Most people want to write fiction. Don't overlook other areas: nonfiction (especially), poetry, plays.

• Pick an issue and give it a kid's eye view. Many publishers are looking for a kid's perspective on peer pressure, the environment, music, movies, etc.

• Get involved with a school publication or start your own.

• Look for opportunities to write. Has something made you mad? Write a letter to the editor of your local paper, a company, or a government office. Have a special friend? Try giving her something that you've written instead of a present. And write as many letters as you can. Friends love to get letters, and you can practice describing things at the same time.

• Read, read, read. When you read a book you like, write down what you like about it. Think about the characters in the novel and how they might have been different if the plot had developed differently. Look at the way that your favorite books begin.

• Be true to what you've written. Don't let anyone tell you that writing isn't important. And don't believe anyone when they tell you you'll never be published, you won't be famous, or you won't make lots of money. You've written what you believe in. Believe in yourself too.

CHAPTER TWO

REVISING, REWRITING, AND PROOFREADING

When you've finished something—whether you've just cleaned your room, learned a new piece on the piano, created a beautiful painting, or done something else spectacular—you probably want to show it off right away. After all, you've just put your heart and soul into something; you're desperate to know what other people think about your accomplishment.

The same is true with writing. After writers have written something that they are really pleased with, they want to share it with anyone who will listen—especially friends, teachers, and publishers. And most serious writers know when they've written something really wonderful. Even professional writers want to get a response right away.

But serious writers fight the urge to send something to a publisher or to share something they've written immediately after it's finished. It's not easy, but serious writers train themselves to wait for a period of time and then to sit down to revise their work. It's one of a writer's most difficult tasks, but it's also one of the most important.

How does this all-important work of revision get done? What are the steps? And how do you know when you've completed them to satisfaction?

This chapter will help you answer those questions so that your work can be as strong as possible. But remember, revision isn't easy, even for writers who have been writing for a long time. Many writers find that revision is more difficult than the process of writing. In spite of that, serious writers revise and revise and revise. They know that revising is the only way that they can be sure that their work is the best that it can be.

STEP ONE: WAIT AWHILE

The good news is that the first step in the revision process is the easiest one. After you've completed a work—even if you feel it's a masterpiece—the best thing to do is to put it away and try not to think about it for awhile. You might try even putting the manuscript—and any books or other tools that you might have used to create the manuscript—completely out of sight. Then move on to something else—a new masterpiece, some poems you've been dying to finish, or just a long letter that you owe a friend. Try your hardest to forget about the piece that you've just written.

Why is it so important to put a piece of work away for a while? There are several reasons.

First of all, you may be "too close" to the manuscript. You've probably worked hard on the story for long periods of time. You may not be able to see either large problems with structure or small mistakes like typos because you've been working on it so long. If you give yourself time away from the manuscript, you will no doubt come back to what you've written, fresh and with what writers call a "new set of eyes."

Secondly, it's difficult to take advice or criticism from others about your work when you are feeling so close to it. An important part of the revision process is asking a second reader—a friend, fellow writer, or trusted adult—for their reaction to your work. If you've just completed that story or poem, you are probably feeling pretty close to it. In fact, if it's fiction, you may feel as if you've actually become one of the characters you've written about. Your second reader will probably make constructive suggestions about your story or poem. If you are feeling "too close" to what you've written, you may take these suggestions a bit too personally, or even as insults, even if they are good, solid suggestions. Then you'll both end up feeling badly about the whole revision process.

How long do you need to wait? Most writers wait at least two weeks before they return to a piece of work that they've completed. Others wait longer and some can simply allow a story to "cool" over a couple of nights. While you need to find the time frame that works best for you and your writing, I recommend between two and and six weeks.

STEP TWO: READ YOUR WORK AGAIN

After you've allowed your manuscript a "cooling off period," it's time to take it out again and give it another read. Read through the story or poem once, with fresh eyes, and see if you still think it's as strong as you did when you put it away. If you're like most writers, you'll think that the work has potential, but you will probably see some problems that you didn't notice the first time.

As you read, try making notes in the margins about some of the problems that you see. If you've handwritten your manuscript, use a different color pen than the one that you've used to write the manuscript to indicate where you'll want to go back and rework a passage here and there. (Most writers use red, but I prefer purple—it's friendlier!)

After you've given your work another read and noted your impressions, try reading it out loud (to any empty room) to test how the work actually sounds. Do the words roll off your tongue nicely or are there places where your tongue trips on something? Does the rhythm sound right or do certain stanzas just sound "off"? Are there pauses in the appropriate places? Do your paragraphs end and begin just right? Does your opening grab the reader? Does your ending sum up your message and tie up any loose ends? Again, make notes on your manuscript so that you'll know what you need to go back and rewrite.

Finally, before you go any further, give the manuscript one last careful read for technical problems. Look for spelling errors, punctuation problems, typos, that sort of thing. If you have a computer with a spell check or grammar check, run the manuscript through the program one last time. Then look at the hard copy again and make sure that you've caught as much as you can.

STEP THREE: REVISE AND REWRITE

Now it's time to get to work and correct, rewrite, massage, and rework some of the passages that you feel are just not quite as good as they can be. At this point, you may throw entire scenes or characters out of your story. You may get rid of whole stanzas or find that you need to add a few more so that your reader will understand a poem's meaning. You might find that your plot doesn't seem logical or that it moves way too quickly toward the end (maybe you were hurrying to get it done). Whatever you find, now's the time to take a hard look at these kinds of problems and correct them.

You might find that there are only minor problems here and there in your work and that you can whip the manuscript into shape pretty easily. But don't be too easy on yourself. It's best to be a little over-critical during this stage of the revision process. Even if you don't rewrite much of the work, make sure that you've reviewed every word, thought about every character, checked each plot twist, and double-checked your grammar, punctuation, and spelling.

Then reread the whole manuscript again—both out loud and silently—to make sure that you caught everything. Pay particular attention to passages that you have rewritten to make sure that you haven't introduced any additional problems or errors.

STEP FOUR: GETTING FEEDBACK

At some point in the revision process, most serious writers ask for feedback from someone else about their work. You can ask for feedback at any stage of the writing process, of course, but you may find it most valuable after you've corrected all the errors and completed all the rewriting. In other words, now that your story, poem, or article is as good as you think it can be, it's time to get someone else's opinion—before you send it off to the publisher.

Who do you ask? The best "second readers" meet several qualifications.

First of all, your second reader needs to be someone whose opinion you value. You should feel confident that the advice they give you is valuable and thought out—even if you don't end up taking it.

Secondly, your second reader should be someone who takes your writing seriously. Your second reader should understand what your writing goals are and should know if publishing your work is one of those goals.

Lastly, and most importantly, your second reader should be comfortable being honest about your work. Your second reader should be the kind of person who gives both negative and positive feedback. And, as a writer, you need to be comfortable with the fact that your second reader may criticize your work.

Who should you choose as your second reader? A good second reader might be another young writer like yourself who takes the writing process seriously. It may also be someone just a bit older than you—in a higher grade—who, because of experience, has a bit more writing advice to offer. You may also ask a teacher or a librarian or even a writer in your community to look at your writing. There may be an adult in your community who is an editor of some kind, perhaps of a newspaper, magazine, or brochures. Professional editors usually give solid and insightful advice—and they know how to give advice in a way that is entirely constructive. (They may not give advice for free, though, so make sure you ask. If they do charge a fee, you'll want to know exactly what that fee is and what kind of evaluation you can expect.)

You may also be able to work a "swap" with a second reader. Perhaps the second reader writes herself and needs a young person's opinion of what she's written. Then you can put your own editor's cap on and get to work!

Be cautious about asking someone who is very close to you—a family member, for instance—to be your second reader. Your mother or father might be very proud of your work, but they may be so proud of what you've done that they have difficulty finding fault with it. Of course, you'll want to share your work with the people who love you and who you care about. Be sure, though, that you understand that the advice that they give may be affected by their feelings towards you.

Should you have more than one second reader? It's always a good idea to get more than one outside opinion about your work. Be careful, though, about asking too many people for advice. You may get so many conflicting messages that you won't be able to take your manuscript in any one direction!

Many serious writers rely on the help that they get from their own writer's group. The members of writer's groups critique and react to each other's works. They also share tidbits about the publishing world, celebrate successes, and share helpful hints. For more information about forming a writers group—and an up-close view of a writer's group in action—see Chapter Three.

When you ask either your writer's group or a second reader for their advice, you may want to ask them to answer a series of questions about your work. By asking them several questions about how they feel about various elements of your manuscript, you can be sure that you are getting the reaction that you feel you need. (You'll find a list of sample questions on page 14.) You may want to add a few questions of your own that hone in on some of the trouble spots you've been working on. Is dialogue a problem for you? Ask your second reader if they find the dialogue natural-sounding. Is rhyme something you have difficulty with? Ask your writer's group if the rhyme sounds forced in various places.

On the other hand, you may just want a simple reaction from your reader. The questions you provide them may point out something that may not actually be a problem. Before you ever ask for feedback, you need to decide the kind of feedback that you want and the amount of detail you need.

STEP FIVE: FINAL REVISION

After you have gathered feedback from your writer's group or your second reader, you're ready to bring the draft to its final form. Make sure that you've considered all of the feedback you've been given, even if you haven't made the decision to revise based on what was said. Then make the changes that you want to make. Remember, it's your story and you need to trust your own judgment and feelings about what you've written.

Finally, read it aloud one last time to check the flow and feel of the story. You might have a friend read it aloud to you so that you can get another view of the story.

You might also want to "test" your story out on an audience. If you have written a story for younger children, for instance, you might want to have it read aloud to a preschool or to a class of kids in a younger grade. Rather than read the story yourself, ask a teacher or a friend to read it for you. Then you can watch the reaction of your audience and see if you are getting the responses you had hoped for. (It's often best to avoid mentioning that you are the author, at least at first. Many children will be so impressed to meet a real-live author that they won't be as critical with the story as they might be otherwise.)

STEP SIX: PROOFREAD!

You've probably been catching typos and spelling mistakes every time that you reviewed your work. Your second reader or writing group has probably pointed out a few too. Now double- and triple-check your work one last time. You may have introduced additional errors when you revised your story. Or an error may have slipped through every single time you've read the piece.

Often, errors or typos that are the most obvious are missed. Double-check your story's title, for instance, or any subheadings. And be sure to check your name, address, and telephone number!

Many writers find it helpful to read their work backwards to catch mistakes. You might want to try this technique. It allows you to look at your work a different way—and that's often when you spot that glaring mistake or error.

And it's always best to have a second set of "eyes" proofread your work after you've done it several times yourself. You might want to ask an older friend, an adult, or just someone you know who is a whiz at this sort of thing. Make sure that they understand that they are simply proofreading at this point—looking for errors in spelling, punctuation, paragraph indents, that sort of thing. At this stage, you should be completely satisfied with all of the basic elements of your story.

After you've finished, sit back and take a little time to relax. Congratulate yourself! Celebrate! You've just completed one of the most difficult stages of the writing process. And you're ready to move ahead and submit your work for publication.

SAMPLE QUESTIONS FOR A SECOND READER

1. Does the opening paragraph make you want to keep reading?

2. Is the middle suspenseful? Does it flow? Does it drag in any places? Do the episodes in the middle develop the characters and the problem?

3. Is the ending effective? Is there a way I could make it more satisfying? Does it fit in with the story's beginning?

4. Do you care about the main character?

5. Does the conflict still make sense? Is it strong enough?

6. Is the story logical?

7. Does the timing make sense?

8. Is the language stiff? Am I too wordy?

9. Are the characters described consistently?

10. Does the story jump around too much? Are there enough transitions, or story bridges, to remind the readers where they are in terms of time and place?

Revision Checklist

__ Have you waited at least two weeks after completing your manuscript to begin revising?

__ Have you given your manuscript a silent read and noted any problems?

— Have you read your manuscript out loud?

__ Have you carefully checked for technical problems? Be sure to check for:

> __ wordiness

> __ grammar problems

> __ spelling problems

> __ punctuation

> __ paragraph indents (Look especially at your dialogue.)

> __ tense changes (Your story should all be in the same tense. Past tense is preferred.)

— Have you rewritten and revised the manuscript to correct any problems?

__ Have you asked for feedback from someone else?

— Have you reacted to the feedback and made one final revision?

— Have you proofread the manuscript one last time? Have you made sure to check the "big stuff" as well as the small details?

__ Has a second reader double-checked your work?

Some Common Errors

1. Capitalize "mom," "dad," "grandma," etc., when used *in place* of a proper name. Example:

When I asked Mom if I could go, she said no.

When I asked my mom if I could go, she said no.

2. When punctuating dialogue, the punctuation mark goes inside the quotation marks.

    "Mom, can I go?" she asked.

    "Mom, I want to go," she said.

3. When a character is using inner dialogue or thinking in segments that sound like dialogue, use italics or underline.

    She just has to let me go, I begged silently.
    It's not fair. Everyone else gets to go, I thought.

4. Begin a new paragraph every time a different character speaks or uses inner dialogue.

5. Don't overuse capitalization. Seasons aren't capitalized, nor are most "general" places. Look it up. If you are still in doubt, leave it lowercase.

CHAPTER THREE

IS A WRITER'S GROUP FOR YOU?

Many serious writers find it helpful to join or start a writer's group. There are many different kinds of writer's groups, but most of them involve a small group of serious writers who gather together to share their writing, compare notes, and celebrate successes.

Why do writers find writer's groups so helpful? Writer's groups are a great source of feedback. Getting opinions from people with similar writing goals can frequently help writers revise their work effectively.

Many writers also use writer's groups to keep them disciplined about their writing. They find that they can stick to their writing schedule if they are expected to share their writing at an upcoming meeting.

Writer's groups can also be a great way to share ideas about the writing process. Members may also share any marketing tips they know or anything they've learned from their publishing research.

Finally, writer's groups are just a great way to socialize. Writing can be a lonely task, and a writer's group meeting is sometimes just an excuse to get together with writers and talk about writing. It's also a great opportunity to celebrate writing successes among "writing friends" who understand what those successes mean.

WHERE DO YOU START?

There may already be an existing writer's group in your community that you can join. Most newspapers list the meetings of such groups in their weekly calendars. Check these listings and, if phone numbers are included, give the contact person a call to find out if the group is accepting new members.

You may also find notices about writer's groups on the bulletin board of your local library, arts center, or bookstore. If you know other writers in your community, ask them if they are part of a group. You might also ask anyone you know who is involved in the world of writing—your teacher or your librarian, for instance.

If you can't find an existing group to join, start your own! What's the best way to get started?

You will want to start by gathering together writers who, like yourself, take themselves seriously. It may not matter if the writers are the same age or if they write in the same genre. If they have serious writing goals and take what they do seriously, they will probably be valuable members of your group.

Next, you'll want to find a place to meet. Your local library may have a meeting room you can use. Your school may also allow a group like yours to meet after hours. Many bookstores love to have writing groups meet on their premises if they have the facilities. Writers are good readers, after all, and they are usually good bookstore customers too! You can also meet in each other's homes, rotating the meeting each time, if your parents are willing and you have a space in your house where you won't be interrupted.

You may find that some meeting sites require that you have an adult advisor or sponsor. If you don't already have an adult in your life who is interested in helping you with your writing and with this particular group, you might try asking a librarian, a teacher, or a local editor if they would be interested in sponsoring the group. A high school student or a college student may also be willing to take the sponsorship on. And don't forget to check with senior citizen centers. Often, a senior citizen will have the time, energy, experience, and the space to work with young writers.

Make sure that you are clear about what role you want your advisor to take. Do you want her to be an active member of the group, offering advice and constructive criticism? Or do you simply want her to observe the group in action? Your adult sponsor needs to know what is expected of her in terms of time commitment and input from the very start. That will save confusion later on.

How large should your group be? Most writers find that a writer's group functions well when it has between four and ten members. That way everyone has the time to make a contribution. Many writers also find the group works best if most of the writers are around the same level in their writing development. If you have already had a few pieces published, for instance, you may feel frustrated if a beginning writer joins your group. On the other hand, new writers frequently have new ideas, and you may discover that this writer can make a valuable contribution—as long as he takes what he is doing seriously.

WHAT DO YOU DO AT A MEETING?

Most writer's groups spend at least part or all of their meeting time critiquing each other's work. Often, a member will stand and read a work aloud and ask for feedback.

Other groups find it more effective to have the writer copy the work and give it to the other members of the group before the meeting. That way, members will have had a chance to read and respond to it before it's read aloud.

Many groups begin their meeting with a reading from an established writer—sometimes a classic piece about the writing process itself. Other groups start by sharing good news. After all, one of your goals is to celebrate each other's successes. You might celebrate something major—like a member getting a piece published—or something minor—like simply getting a manuscript completed and submitted to a publisher. Either way, it's good to get a pat on the back—and it will probably give you a good feeling to support other writers who are successful too.

Some writer's groups have a "program" at some or all of their meetings. They may invite a published writer, an editor, or some other publishing professional to the group to discuss writing or publishing. This is a great way to learn more about the real world of writing and publishing. If you do invite a speaker, ask if they require a fee. If they are willing to speak for free, make sure to offer them a small token of your appreciation. It may be a copy of your group's literary magazine, for instance, or something as simple as a bouquet of flowers you've picked from your yard. You need to do something to demonstrate to them that you know that their time is valuable and that you appreciate what they've had to offer. Make sure to follow up with a thank you note too.

Other groups have found it valuable to include a publishing professional as an occasional group member, asking for their input along with the input of the other members of the group. You may want to go this route, saving time at the end of the session for questions and discussion.

Whatever you decide about the content of your meetings, be sure and set a meeting schedule that is fairly regular. You may decide to meet on the first Tuesday of every month for instance. You may feel you need to meet more frequently. Most successful writer's groups meet either every other week or once a month for a couple hours at the most.

THE GROUND RULES FOR CONSTRUCTIVE CRITICISM

It's not easy to accept criticism. That's why it's important to always give your friends comments in a constructive way—a way that will help them to improve their writing. Remember that it soon will be your turn to get that same criticism. Think about the way that you would like to hear criticism of your work.

Criticism is best if it is specific. Instead of saying something like, "I don't like the story," let the writer know what parts you didn't like. Was it the characters, the plot, the setting? Is the story's structure simply too complicated? Are there so many technical problems that the story's true meaning doesn't come through?

And criticism is always easier to take if you combine it with some praise. Instead of saying that you felt the poem was corny, for instance, you might say, "I like what you are trying to get across in the poem. I wonder if there are some new and fresher ways to get across the feelings you describe."

It might help to begin by establishing some ground rules for criticism. As a group, you might agree, for instance, never to laugh out loud or to make fun of each other's work. You might also agree to limit the discussion of a single piece of work to 10 or 15 minutes, so that the criticism doesn't drag on and get overwhelming. You may agree that every group member should come up with one compliment and one criticism of the piece being discussed.

Another way to keep the group functioning smoothly and to make sure that everyone is involved equally is to rotate the chairperson of the meeting. At each meeting, a different person should take over the responsibility of running the group and of keeping the meeting moving smoothly. That way, no one feels as if he or she is in charge of the group or should be controlling what is going on.

Whatever structure you find works for you, remember that egos can sometimes get in the way. Do your best to be fair and kind to your group's members and to make sure that everyone has a voice. Your adult sponsor may be willing to help you out with this.

HOW TO TELL IF YOUR WRITING GROUP IS WORKING

Every once in awhile, you'll want to take a hard look at your group and make sure that it is doing what it is supposed to do—support your writing.

Sometimes writers find that they have moved ahead of other members of their group. Some members of your group may still be struggling with the basic techniques, while you have moved ahead to more complicated ones. Don't be embarrassed about your success. It may be time to move on to another writing group or to seek out some other means of support—a special class, or workshop, for instance.

You may also find that several egos are taking over the group. Again, this may be a signal that the group is no longer for you. If the feedback that you are getting isn't valuable or if it is given in a mean-spirited way, it's time to leave the group or disband it! You have better things to do—like work on your writing.

And speaking of working on your writing, be sure that you are getting enough writing done. If your meetings are eating into your writing time, it's time to stop going to those meetings! Your time is best spent writing and revising. Don't use your meetings as an excuse to keep you away from the serious business of writing.

Writer's groups aren't for everybody. While many writers find them helpful, some writers simply don't feel that they are a valuable way to spend their time. You need to decide for yourself whether a writing group is for you and which kind of writing group is most helpful to your writing.

A WRITER'S GROUP THAT WORKS:
THE RASPBERRY YOUNG WRITER'S GROUP

The Raspberry Writer's Group
by Anne E. Kafoure

I have always been a writer, and thanks to positive encouragement from family and friends, I have always taken my work seriously. However, throughout elementary school and part of middle school, I never had any contact with other people my age who shared my strong passion for writing. I always felt rather alone in my youthful joy of composing stories and poems, until, at age thirteen, I became involved in a teen writer's group at a local bookstore. There I met a dozen young people who possessed amazing talent and shared my love of the written word. I learned a tremendous amount from listening to them, reading my work to them, and taking their suggestions. The monthly meetings were always a wonderful experience. Unfortunately, after less than a year, the supervisor of the group moved away, and, much to my dismay, the meetings ended.

Two years later, when I was fifteen, I was fortunate enough

to sign a publishing contract with Raspberry Publications for my book, **The Whale Dancers.** In an early conversation with the publishers, I happened to mention my old writer's group and how much I missed the inspiration and motivation it had given me. The publishers, Curt Jenkins and Susan Schmidt, seemed interested in the idea of a writer's group for young people and asked me if I would ever want to become involved in another one. I responded with an enthusiastic "yes," and they decided to take the initiative and start their own young writer's group. A few months later, the Raspberry Writer's Group, with members from fifth through twelfth grade, held its first meeting at the Westerville Public Library in Westerville, Ohio. The group was an instant success.

On the second Tuesday of every month, the dozen or so members gather at 7:00PM in the library meeting room. We each bring poetry, a story, or an article that we are working on, and we take turns reading our work to the group. The group members then offer suggestions, comments, compliments, and constructive criticism to the author. We continue in this manner until everyone has a chance to share their work. This process has helped every member in the group make improvements in both writing and presentation skills.

However, the benefits of the Raspberry Writer's Group do not stop there. In addition to our dozen regular members, every month Susan Schmidt brings in a different local published author to our meetings. They, too, offer suggestions to individual members of the group about specific compositions and also answer questions about writing and publishing in general. We have been fortunate enough to meet and talk with novelists, poets, children's authors, magazine and newspaper editors and journalists, free-lance writers, proofreaders, and more. I have learned a tremendous amount from these visiting professionals about their careers, writing styles, etc., and I have also gained a great deal by listening to every talented member of the group, whether they are eleven or seventeen. I feel that our Raspberry Writer's Group has a comfortable atmosphere of encouragement and support, and that we have become like a little family of hopeful writers already beginning to make our mark in the world. And I'm not the only one who is reaping the joys and benefits of the Raspberry Writer's Group; here are some of the comments other group members have made:

"I enjoy it. I always look forward to it."

"The age range is good; we all have different views and different experiences."

"The older kids can help the younger kids to expand and think, while the younger kids can help the older kids with basics that they've missed."

"And we aren't competitive because of our variety of ages. We're all at different levels. Actually, it's hard to imagine a group that would be competitive."

"You have to keep an open mind. You can't have prejudices and expect to get along."

"My favorite part of the group is the visiting author."

"It's good to get a critique from someone who has their work out there and is used to criticism."

"They (the visiting authors) are used to giving and receiving criticism."

"I like the visiting author, too. It gives us an insight as to what we're all getting ourselves into."

"I've developed my reading skills."

"I've gained respect for all kinds of writing."

"Listening to other people's writing has made me aware of skills they have that I lack, like details, descriptions, etc., and so it helps me better those skills in my writing."

"I gain ideas from listening to other people's work."

"The group has forced me to open up."

"I've learned to take advice—all it can do is help."

"It's nice, after you read your work, to have people respect you."

That respect is what makes the Raspberry Writer's Group so successful. We respect the visiting authors, the other group members, ourselves, and we have learned to respect the writing of everyone in the group, taking it seriously and forming a helpful atmosphere where all can learn and grow.

CHAPTER FOUR

HOW TO SUBMIT YOUR MANUSCRIPT TO A PUBLISHER

You're finally there! You've written a wonderful piece, let it "rest," and then revised it. You've proofread it and had a friend double-check your proofreading. You're satisfied with your work, your writing group loves it, and your teacher is excited about where you might go from here. So, what's the next step? How do you get it published?

STEP ONE: DO YOUR RESEARCH HOMEWORK

Your job as a serious writer is to get your manuscript into the hands of a publishing company—but not just any publishing company. You need to find a publishing company that publishes the kind of piece that you've written.

That's where research comes in. There are a number of important tools that can make your research a little bit easier.

The first tool is right at your fingertips—it's this book! The second section lists magazine and book publishers, what they are publishing now and what they plan to publish in the future. You'll find their targeted age group, the categories of books or articles they publish, their submission requirements, and other guidelines. You'll also find information about contests for young writers: their requirements, deadlines, the prizes they offer, and whether they offer publication as part of their award.

Take some time to browse through the listings right now and think about the manuscript or manuscripts you have revised and ready to go. Then choose three or four likely publishers for your work.

Besides this book, some of the best sources of information about publishers are writer's guidelines. Most publishing companies and magazines publish their own writer's guidelines, a summary of what they are publishing, what new lines of books or articles they are introducing, their requirements, helpful hints on how to make sure that your writing is appropriate for them, and more. How do you get writer's guidelines? It's easy! Simply sit down and write a letter to the publishers requesting them and include a self-addressed stamped envelope (SASE). Your letter can be short and to the point; no need for anything fancy or involved at this point.

(On page 72, you'll find a copy of the writer's guidelines for Raspberry Publications. You'll also find a sample of a letter requesting guidelines from a publishing company on page 36.)

There are a few other research tools that can help you to narrow down publishers too. Your library probably has a copy of a book called *Literary Marketplace* in their reference department. *Literary Marketplace* (LMP for short) lists all of the companies currently publishing books. You'll also find a book called *The Writer's Market*. Take a look at these resources and see what else they can tell you about the publishing companies that you have selected.

A number of magazines can also supply you with information about publishing opportunities. *Writer's Digest, Writer's Journal,* and *The Writer* all have up-to-date information about publishers' needs. *Publishers Weekly,* the magazine of the publishing industry, frequently provides similar information.

Another way to find out more about publishing opportunities is to attend writer's conferences. Most large cities, and many smaller towns, have writer's conferences that may be sponsored by local colleges, writer's groups, or other organizations. At a writer's conference, you can meet other writers like yourself, listen to speakers talk about writing and marketing, and, sometimes, meet editors or agents who may be part of the "real world" of publishing. Most writer's conferences charge a fee and some can be expensive. If you find yourself short of cash, call the organization that is sponsoring the conference and ask if they have a reduced student rate. You could also ask if they would be willing to waive the fee if you worked at the conference or helped out with pre-conference mailings or publicity.

Finally, the best way to find out what a publishing company or magazine is publishing is to read the magazines yourself or to check out the other books the publisher has published. You can probably find copies of magazines that publish works by young writers in your local library. Take a little time to read them and to think about the poems, stories, and essays that they feature. Then ask yourself if the piece that you have written fits well with the other kinds of things they've published. If you have written a book, look for other books published by the publisher you've selected. Does your manuscript seem to fit in with what else they've published?

Now that you've done your research homework, it's time to double-check yourself to make sure that you've chosen the appropriate publisher for your work. Take a look at the research checklist below and make sure that your manuscript meets the publisher's requirements.

• Does the publisher you've chosen publish other articles, stories, or books about the subject matter you are writing about?

• Does the publisher publish other works that are the same type or genre as your piece? (In other words, if your story is a fantasy, does this particular publisher publish fantasy?)

• Is your work written for the age group that the publisher is appealing to?

• Does the length of your work match the publisher's requirements?

Test Market Your Idea—Write a Query Letter

A query letter is a letter that a writer writes to an editor to ask if they are interested in a specific story or article idea. Most publishers prefer to see entire manuscripts from young writers. A few, though, ask a young writer to write a query letter describing the story idea first.

A query letter can save you lots of time and postage. It's a way to "test-market" your idea on an editor before you even write it or send it out.

You'll find an example of a query letter on page 38. You'll notice that a query contains the information that the publisher needs to know, but is written in a way that tempts the editor. Your goal in a query letter is to get an editor excited about the piece you've written—so much so, that she wants to see the final product.

STEP TWO: THE MANUSCRIPT PACKAGE

When it's time to send your manuscript off to a publisher, you want to put your best foot forward. That means putting together a manuscript package that shows a publisher that you are serious about writing and about having your work published.

A manuscript package includes the following elements:
- A cover letter
- The manuscript itself
- A self-addressed stamped envelope (SASE)
- A reply card (optional)

Since your manuscript is the most important part of this package, let's talk about that first. How should your manuscript look when you send it off to a publisher?

Serious writers type their manuscripts on a computer or a typewriter. Manuscripts should always be double-spaced, with wide margins. They should be free of errors and any mistakes that you have found during proofreading should be corrected by the typewriter or computer, not in ink by hand. You should use good quality paper. And, if you are using a word processor with a dot matrix printer, make sure that the type is dark enough to be read.

Some publishers *do* accept handwritten manuscripts. Their

listing in this book or their writer's guidelines will tell you their requirements. If they do accept handwritten manuscripts, make sure that your printing is readable and that you used lined paper. And, keep in mind, that even if they do accept handwritten submissions, a typewritten or word-processed manuscript always looks more professional.

The first page of your fiction or nonfiction manuscript should include your name, address, and phone number (optional) in the upper left-hand corner. You can also include your social security number or your date of birth if you wish. In the right- hand corner, you should include the approximate length of your manuscript in number of words. (Many word processing programs calculate this automatically for you.)

The title should appear about midway down the first page of the manuscript. No page number should appear on the first page.

The rest of the manuscript can be typed starting at the top of the page, but be sure to leave at least a one inch margin. You'll also want to be sure that the rest of your manuscript pages are numbered. (For a sample of manuscript form, turn to page 34.)

If you are submitting poetry, you should type the poem exactly as you want it to appear, single-spaced, with double spaces between stanzas. Center the poem on the page and include only one poem per page. Put your name, address, and telephone number, social security number, and date of birth (the last three items are optional) at the top of each page.

When you submit illustrations to a publisher, make sure you protect them with a fixative or cover them with a sheet of tissue paper to keep the colors from rubbing off onto another page. You will probably want to slide a piece of cardboard in between your drawings to keep them from being bent in the mail.

Your cover letter is the second most important part of your manuscript package. In your cover letter, you are simply introducing yourself to the editor who will be reading your work and telling them a little bit about your manuscript.

It's always best to address your cover letter and the envelope that you mail your package in to a specific editor. You can find out the names of editors in the listings in the second half of this book or from the writer's guidelines.

What kinds of things should you include in your cover letter? Your opening paragraph should get right to the point. Tell the editor what you are sending them, the title of the manuscript you've enclosed, and what genre it is—poetry, story, essay, etc. You can also include a line or two about what the piece of writing is about.

In your second paragraph, you should tell the publisher a little bit about yourself—your writing experience, your publishing record, your age (if you wish), and any special writing classes that you've taken.

Your last paragraph should express appreciation to the editor for considering your work. You may also mention that you are happy to revise the work if the editor wishes. And, finally, ask that your manuscript be returned if it is not suitable for the publisher in the SASE that you've enclosed. (For a sample cover letter, see page 37.)

Now let's talk about that SASE. Your self-addressed stamped envelope should include your name and address both as the return address and in the sender spot. The appropriate postage should be in place on the envelope. (When you take your manuscript to the post office to be mailed off, simply ask for the same amount of postage and attach it to your SASE.) You may fold your SASE when you place it in your manuscript package.

Some writers don't include a SASE at all and suggest that the publisher can throw out the manuscript if they can't publish it. If you are low on finances, you might consider this option. Take the time to think about the message that this sends to the publisher, though. You are actually suggesting that the publisher throw out your manuscript. That's a pretty negative message about how you feel about your own work.

To make sure that your manuscript arrived at the publishing house or magazine, you might want to include a reply card. Address the card to yourself and ask that the publisher mail it back to you once they've received the manuscript. You'll find a sample reply card on page 39.

STEP THREE: KEEPING RECORDS

Just after you've submitted a manuscript to a publisher, you need to record where you've sent it and when. Keeping a manuscript log is simple—and it's a good way for serious writers to keep track of their work. You'll find a sample manuscript log on page 112. You'll want to review your manuscript log at least once a week to make sure that you know where your manuscripts are and how long they are being held.

STEP FOUR: WAITING

Now it's time to play the waiting game. How long do you have to wait? The writer's guidelines will sometimes tell you the amount of time that a publisher typically takes to review a manuscript. It may take as long as three months—or longer. After you've mailed a manuscript off, it's best to move on to something new and at least try not to let the waiting game take over your writing life!

If you haven't heard from a publisher in three months time, try dropping them a line and asking—nicely of course—if they have had a chance to review your manuscript. It's important to be tactful. This isn't the time to threaten to take the manuscript to another publisher or to express your impatience. Instead, adopt a friendly "just checking in" tone. You'll find a sample follow-up letter on page 40.

STEP FIVE: THE ANSWER!

If you've written your best work, done your research homework, and put together a manuscript package correctly, you may just get rewarded! You may hear that a publisher wants to publish your work!

Some book publishers give the news by phone. Other publishers let you know through the mail. Either way you hear, it will probably be one of the most exciting moments of your life!

After that giddy feeling wears off and you've made all of those important phone calls to your friends, relatives, and teachers, it's time to get down to the details of publishing—and that means thinking about your publishing contract.

Book publishers will either offer you a flat fee contract or royalty contract, with an advance. A flat fee means that they pay you a one-time fee for the right to publish your work. A royalty means that they give you a percentage of the price of each book sold. An advance is an amount of money that they pay you up front that they will deduct from your royalties later on. Sound confusing? It is—even adult writers sometimes have trouble understanding it. The important thing to remember is that serious writers are paid for their work. You may be so thrilled to be published that you might think you should "do it for free." But think again! You're serious about what you do and you deserve to be paid for it.

Magazine publishers handle contracts differently than book publishers do. They may not pay for your services at all (their writer's guidelines should state this) or they may pay you in free copies. Some pay a small fee for your work.

With a magazine publisher, you need to be very clear about who *owns* your work. Most magazines want "all rights" to the work, which means that they have the right to reprint your story or poem or article as many times as they want—and you cannot send it any place else. If you can, it's best to offer a magazine "one-time rights" which means you can resell the article to another magazine after it's been published elsewhere. (You'll find more information on rights in the glossary.)

If you're like most serious writers, you will probably receive rejection slips instead of acceptance. If you do receive a rejection slip, don't despair! All writers—even the most famous writers you can think of—received rejection slips before they finally "made it."

It may help you to think about what a rejection slip *is*. A rejection slip simply says that the publisher cannot use your work at the present time. They may have published a book or article like it. It may not fit in with their publishing plan. Or they may simply have too many stories or manuscripts to publish.

Now let's think about what a rejection slip is *not*. A rejection slip is not a rejection of you or of your writing. When a publisher sends you a rejection slip, he is not telling you that your writing isn't any good or that you'll never achieve success. He's not saying that you are a bad person or a bad writer. He's just saying that he can't publish your work at this particular time. It's that simple.

Here's another thought—when you receive a rejection slip it's proof that someone took your work seriously enough to consider it.

More than that, though, a rejection slip shows that *you* are serious about your writing. After all, you actually submitted it to a publisher. That's a huge step, one that many adult writers can't bring themselves to take. So if your manuscript has been rejected, congratulations!

MANUSCRIPT FORMAT—fiction and nonfiction

Your Name

Your Address

Your telephone number (optional)

Your social security number

or date of birth

                                        About XXX words

                            TITLE

                        By Your Name

This is what your fiction or nonfiction manuscript
should look like when you send it off to a publisher.
Your name and address should be at the top of the page.
The approximate length of your manuscript should
appear in the right hand corner. Then skip to about the
middle of your page and type your title in all caps.
Type your name underneath your title. Then skip three
or four spaces and start your story.

Make sure that you double space and use only one side of
the paper. Make sure that the margins are wide too.

You don't need to include a page number on the first
page of your story. On every page after that, you
should put your last name and page number at the top of
the page.

MANUSCRIPT FORMAT—poetry

Your Name
Your Address
Your telephone number (optional)
Your social security number or date of birth

                              TITLE
                          By Your Name

        This is what your poem
        should look like
        when you submit it
        to the publisher.

        You will want to indent an inch or more
        from your left margin.
        Be sure to type only one poem per page.

        Poems can be single spaced, but be
        sure to include double spaces between stanzas.

SAMPLE LETTER REQUESTING WRITER'S GUIDELINES

Your name
Your address

Date

Publishing Company or Magazine
Address

Dear Sir or Madame:

I am writing to request your writer's guidelines. I am
especially interested in publishing opportunities for
young writers.

Could you send me your current guidelines? I have
enclosed a SASE for your convenience.

Thank you. I'll look forward to hearing from you.

Sincerely,

Your Name

SAMPLE COVER LETTER

Your name
Your address

Date

Editor's Name
Publishing Company or Magazine
Address

Dear Editor: *(use their name if you have it)*

I am pleased to enclose my poem, *Summer,* for your
consideration. The poem is fourteen lines long and
captures all of the sights and sounds of the summer
season. It would work well in your June or July issue.

I am in fourth grade at Jones Elementary School and am a
serious writer. I have taken a number of writing
workshops and have been published in the local paper.

If you feel you cannot use my poem, please return it to
me in the enclosed self-addressed stamped envelope.
Thank you for considering my work.

Sincerely,

Your Name

SAMPLE QUERY LETTER

Your name
Your address

Date

Editor's Name
Publishing Company or Magazine
Address

Dear Editor: *(use their name if you have it)*

It seems as if everyone is talking about the environment, but no one is doing anything about it! Your readers might be interested in learning more about one school that took a stand about pollution. Englishtown Elementary adopted a stream in the neighborhood, had the water tested, and organized the clean-up project. Today, the stream can be enjoyed by everyone in the community.

Would you be interested in an article about how the students at Englishtown did this? I have completed a 500-word essay about the experience and would be happy to send it to you for your consideration. I also could provide photographs of some of the clean up activities.

I am in the fourth grade at Englishtown Elementary and am a serious writer. I enjoy writing about the environment and nature and have been published in our school's literary magazine.

I have enclosed a SASE for your response. Thank you for considering my idea for an article.

Sincerely,

Your Name

SAMPLE REPLY CARD

_____(editor's name) received the story, (Title of your story), on_____(date).

(The front of the postcard should be addressed to you.)

Sample Follow-up Letter

```
                          Your name
                        Your address

    Date

    Editor's Name
    Publishing Company or Magazine
    Address

    Dear Ms. Editor:

    I am writing for information about my manuscript. In
    July, I sent you a story, "The Best Dog in the World." I
    was wondering if you have had a chance to review it yet?

    Could you let me know at your earliest convenience? I
    have enclosed a SASE for your reply. Thank you.

    Sincerely,


    Your Name
```

CHAPTER FIVE

DON'T OVERLOOK THESE MARKETS

Finding the path to publication is sometimes like following the clues in a complicated mystery. So far you've probably uncovered some important clues through the research that you've done in Chapter Four. You've probably considered a couple of different kinds of publishing opportunities for your work—book publishers and magazines or journals that specialize in publishing works by young writers. There are some important clues—or markets—for your work that you may not have thought of. It's important not to overlook these opportunities. They just may be your path to publishing success!

As you are reviewing these "overlooked markets," keep one thing in mind: most writers—both young and old—are interested primarily in publishing fiction, either short stories or novels. The simple truth is that there are more publishing opportunities in nonfiction than fiction. Check out any magazine at your local library. They may carry one—or maybe two—short stories, but the remainder of the magazine is nonfiction. Compare the fiction section of your local book store to the nonfiction section. You'll probably find that the nonfiction section is much, much larger.

Writing nonfiction can be as creative and fun as writing fiction—and just as rewarding! It's a great way to earn a few "publishing credits," (what serious writers refer to as their published works). You'll also find that many publishers will take your fictional work more seriously if you've already published a few nonfiction pieces.

So, with that general advice in mind, let's look at some more clues in this publishing puzzle. Let's consider some overlooked markets that just might be excited about publishing your work:

Local Newspapers

Most communities have at least one major newspaper that comes out every day. Many have one or several weekly papers that cover events and issues that are of concern to your immediate local area.

Make sure that you check out both of these papers for publishing opportunities. Frequently, both daily and weekly papers feature a "kid's page" where young writers actually write some of the articles. Other papers feature "young reporters" who may cover school events or other events that pertain to younger readers. If your papers feature these kinds of articles or pages, give them a call and find out what their guidelines are for becoming a regular writer. And if they don't, drop them a line and ask them if they would be willing to consider adding such a feature. It doesn't hurt to ask! And the paper's editorial staff may love the idea—perhaps they were just waiting to find a willing and able reporter. That's where you come in!

If your local paper isn't able to offer you a position as a reporter, ask about becoming a guest columnist, giving a "kid's-eye" view of something that is going on in the world, in general, or in your community in particular.

Many daily and weekly papers also sponsor writing contests. You may be asked to write on a specific subject, like patriotism, for example, or to submit some of your best work on an unspecified topic. Kids may also be asked to write movie or book reviews as part of a newspaper contest. Keep your eye out for these. They usually have strict deadlines and guidelines. You'll want to make sure that you are submitting the appropriate work, that it is of the right length, and that you have it in on time!

Finally, think about writing a letter to the editor about an issue that you feel strongly about. It's a great way to catch an editor's eye. Most newspaper editors will be impressed that a young person went to the trouble to write at all! And, best of all, you've been able to express yourself about an important issue—and communicated your feelings in print to other members of your community.

What should you write about? Focus on issues in your community that are of particular interest to young people and that are timely. You may want to offer to cover a local sports tournament or to interview the star of your school production. You might want to try something harder hitting—like how kids feel about a landfill in your community, for instance, or how cheating is dealt with at your school. There are lots of possibilities. Ask your friends, spend a little time brainstorming, and jot down some ideas.

You might also want to write about an area that you know something about. Could you review the new educational computer games, for instance? How about a review of your favorite CD or concert? Could you write about bicycling, review roller blade trails, discuss the various hiking facilities in your area?

Alternative Papers

Many communities also have alternative papers, papers that are geared toward entertainment, but also may feature some articles on local politics or community events. These papers usually feature lots of music (both of concerts and CD's) and movie reviews. Again, drop them a note and see if they would consider your perspective on these subjects. And make sure that you tell them why you are qualified to give your opinion. Perhaps you've been following a particular band for a couple of years, for instance. Maybe you are up on all the latest Batman comics and might be the perfect person to see if the movies live up to the traditional comics.

Alternative papers may also be interested in articles about current fads or trends in your community among young people. Think about what kids your age are into and pitch a couple of ideas to an editor of an alternative paper.

And alternative papers may also be willing to offer you the

same opportunities that local papers do—the chance to become a guest columnist or writing regular features on issues of concern to young people.

Parenting Papers and Magazines

Many local communities publish parenting magazines that focus on issues of interest to parents and children in the area. There are also several national magazines that focus on child-rearing and parenting.

What can you offer these magazines or newspapers? Again, as a young person, you have a unique viewpoint. You can offer them a kid's perspective on a number of different topics—and frequently they need a kid's-eye view to round out their coverage of an issue.

Take a look at these publications and see what kinds of issues they are covering. Then write for their guidelines if they are available. Next, think of a few ideas to pitch to them that fit their guidelines and reflect your unique perspective as a young person.

Stuck for ideas? Here are a few to get you started:
- What It's Really Like to be Homeschooled—by a Kid Who's Been There!
- How to Make the Most of Your Babysitter
- What Are Magic Cards All About Anyway?
- What Kids Really Want to Know About Politics
- How Much Pressure is Too Much Pressure?
- What Kids Really Think About Joint Custody

Newsletters

If you have a special hobby, interest, or are involved in a sport, you may already receive a newsletter about the topic. Newsletters are always looking for writers, especially writers who are experts on the subject! And, once again, you can offer them a fresh and unique perspective.

Are you into chess? There are a number of newsletters, both national and local, on chess events. How about the Civil War?

Short wave radio? Gymnastics? Computers? Name a topic—there's probably a newsletter that covers the subject in detail.

Where do you find out about newsletters? Check out your local library and ask the reference librarian for a copy of the *Encyclopedia of Associations.* It's a large volume that lists various organizations by their subject of interest and any newsletters and publications they may publish. Then write for their guidelines or send them a query letter. You just might be the writer they are looking for.

Religious Publications

There are a large number of publications that serve the religious community. They range from large publishing houses like Thomas Nelson and the Jewish Publication Society to smaller operations that publish for Sunday schools. There are also smaller publishing companies associated with other religions—like the Bah'ai Publishing Trust. And there are a number of magazines that serve the religious market, like *Guideposts for Kids, Breakaway,* and *Brio.*

Some of these publications and publishing houses accept work from young people, but their needs are generally quite specific. Again, write away for guidelines or query the editors about a specific topic. If you receive a positive response to your query, make sure that you follow through and write the article exactly as you proposed it.

And Don't Forget Puzzles, Games, Jokes

But wait a minute, you're probably thinking. *Am I really a serious writer if I'm writing things like riddles or creating word games and mazes?* While these may seem like gimmicks to you, they are a great way to "break into" print and they frequently pay fairly well.

Best of all, editors are generally desperate for these—especially for games and puzzles. If you have a knack for puzzles, you may just find an easy path to publishing success.

And, once you've published a few of these kinds of things,

you've built your publishing credit list. You've also had the opportunity to develop some rapport with an editor—and that relationship may just serve you well later on when you want to suggest a terrific nonfiction article, submit a fantastic short story or poem.

Remember, the publishing world is full of lots of different opportunities. Solid research, creativity, and a willingness to look at some "nontraditional" markets, will allow you to take full advantage of all of the opportunities out there!

CHAPTER SIX

DO-IT-YOURSELF PUBLISHING

Many serious writers choose to pursue a slightly unusual, different route to having their work published—they choose to do it themselves! With today's technology, it's not a difficult task and it can be quite a rewarding and satisfying route to getting your work into print.

Why do some writers choose to publish their own work instead of seeking a "real" publisher?

Many writers simply want to have total control of their work. They want to decide how it's edited, illustrated, and packaged. They also want to market their own books—either by contacting a bookstore on their own or finding other ways to sell their work.

Some writers have tried traditional publishing houses and have been rejected a number of times. They know their story or book is good and that it has an audience out there. Self-publishing is one way to reach that audience.

Other writers have written a book or a work that is simply too specific for a traditional publisher—a collection of maps of hiking trails in a city park system, for example, or a guide to summer volunteer opportunities for teenagers.

Finally, many writers have written a special work that they want a small number of people to see. They want the opportunity to "customize" their book for their teachers, parents, or grandparents, but they want their work to look professional.

So how do you decide if self-publishing is for you? Here are some practical things to consider.

DO YOU HAVE THE MONEY TO INVEST IN SELF-PUBLISHING?

Depending on the way you decide to publish your work (you'll find more on that later in this chapter), publishing can be an expensive proposition. You may be able to find some sources of funding, though. Your school may offer grant money—through a teacher, perhaps—for publishing student works. Or a particular organization may be so taken with your idea that they offer you a grant or help you with the project.

DO YOU HAVE THE SKILLS TO PUT THE PROJECT TOGETHER?

If you choose to self-publish your own work, you're not just a writer. You're also an editor, proofreader, typesetter, and illustrator. Most successful self-publishing projects are successful because they *look* professional. They look as if a serious writer/editor has put the project together. To make a self-published project work, you need to rely on your skills in these areas or to find someone else in your community who can assist you. The biggest mistake you can make is to create a book that is full of typos or simply poorly constructed. If the book looks unprofessional and sloppy, so will you.

ARE YOU PREPARED TO MARKET YOUR OWN WORK?

If you want your self-published book to reach book buyers, you have to work hard to get it into the hands of bookstore managers. This can be a bit overwhelming. If, on the other hand, you have a specific audience in mind—the libraries in your community, for example, or your fellow classmates—your job may be slightly easier. Either way, though, there is work involved and it's often work that isn't directly related to the writing process. If you take this on, you'll learn a lot about the "real world" of publishing, but you may find yourself pulled in so many directions that you aren't able to focus on writing itself.

If you've made the decision to "self-publish" your work, there are several different directions you can go. Let's look at a few of them:

Vanity Presses

Vanity presses are publishing companies that, for a fee, will take care of all of the details of publishing your book. They'll take on the editing, proofreading, typesetting, binding, printing, and, sometimes, the illustrations. They may also do some limited marketing for you once the book is published.

Vanity Presses can be quite expensive and are looked down on by some members of the publishing community. Still, some writers have achieved success going this route.

Your Local Printing Company

In most communities, there are printing companies that are in the business of printing brochures, pamphlets, catalogs and the like. Some of these companies may be willing to take on a book project—again, for a fee. If you work with a traditional printing company rather than a vanity press, you can probably save a little money. Remember, though, that you'll need to take care of all of the details—like editing and proofreading—yourself.

The cost of printing can often be reduced if you supply the printing company with your manuscript on a computer disk. Be sure to contact them first for their exact requirements.

If you work with a printing house or vanity press, you'll want to ask for an estimate of exactly how much the whole project will cost and an idea of what your end product will look like. Be sure to ask for samples of their work, references, and their billing policies.

Your Local Copy Store

One of the most inexpensive ways to self-publish your work is to visit your local copy store. The price can be especially reasonable if you are planning to produce a small number of copies and if all of the illustrations are in black and white, rather than in color. Many copy stores can actually bind the work and provide you with a heavy cardboard for the cover.

Again, ask for an estimate based on the number of copies you intend to produce and the material they intend to use. And, in preparing your material, be sure that you include all of the necesssary "book" elements—including a title page and a copyright page! Just because you produced the book at a copy store, doesn't mean that it isn't protected by a copyright.

Your Own Computer

If you are producing a small number of copies of a single book or if you want to create a customized book for a friend or relative (one that features them as a main character, for instance, or includes a special chapter or poem meant just for their eyes), you can simply put the book together on your home computer. It's best to have a good quality printer—a laser printer, if possible—so that the type will be dark, readable, and professional-looking. You can either bind it yourself by sewing or stapling it, or take it to your local copy store.

Blank Books and Book Kits

There are a number of book-making kits on the market that provide you with the materials to produce your own books. Some of the kits include the address of a company that will "publish" your work after you've completed the kit. Both of these are terrific options, especially if you create a single copy of a custom-made book.

Bookstores and educational stores also sell "blank books," already bound books that are blank, so that you you can write your own story inside or create your own collection of poems. Again, this is a terrific way to publish your work or to create a special keepsake for a friend or teacher.

A simple sketch pad, a photo album, or a cardboard portfolio can also be used to create your own book—inexpensively! You may want to have the cover "laminated" or covered with clear sticky paper to preserve it. (I still have a collection of poems that I wrote when I was younger called "A little Piece of Me." I created the book from a sketchbook, illustrated the poems with watercolors, and presented the book to my mother on Mother's Day.)

Your Own Literary Magazine

You can use either your local copy store, your home computer, or a traditional printing house to create your own literary magazine! This can be a terrific project for your writing group. It allows every member of your group to break into print. And it gives you all something to work for!

If you decide to create your own literary magazine, make sure you make some decisions before you even get started.

First of all, consider your budget for the magazine. In coming up with a budget, you need to think about whether you will include photographs or illustrations, whether they will be in color or black and white, exactly how long the magazine will be, and how many copies you will print. Then contact your local copy store or printer and ask them to quote a price. Perhaps your school has a copy machine or print shop that you can use for free or at minimal cost. Even so, you need to make some decisions about the length, number of copies, and what kinds of things you will include.

Next, you need to find out where the money is coming from. Perhaps members of your writer's group can raise funds for the project. Maybe you can all contribute a certain amount. Then, if you decide to sell the magazine instead of giving it away, you can split the profits.

Next, you need to decide exactly what kinds of submissions you will include. Do you want to include just poetry? Poetry and short stories? Poetry, short stories, and essays? Who will make the final decision about what you will include?

And then, of course, you need to put the entire magazine together. You'll end up with a more professional-looking magazine if you use a single computer and the same typeface for every piece. Be sure to include all of the important elements, once again: a title page, table of contents, and a copyright page. You might even want to include a list of contributors, with their photographs, and an index of first lines and titles.

As for getting your magazine out there, contact local bookstores to see if they might carry it on "consignment." (They will pay you if it sells.) Educational stores are also a likely market. And, of course, your local library and school library will no doubt want to add a copy to their collection.

Do-it-yourself publishing? Why not! It just might be the best way for you to break into print for the first time. And you'll learn all about the publishing process as you do just that.

CHAPTER SEVEN

YOUR FUTURE AS A WRITER

Now that you know what it means to be a serious young writer, you may be wondering what your future holds. What is the world going to be like when you are a serious adult writer? What opportunities are out there? What obstacles will you encounter? Can you really support yourself with a career in writing?

THE WRITER'S ROLE IN THE WORLD

Since you are a writer, you know how powerful the written word is, you know that words can make people think, can convince them to change their minds, can spur them to action, and can move them emotionally.

That's why you need to take your role as a writer very seriously. You have the opportunity to change the world with your words. It's an awesome responsibility and you shouldn't take it lightly. Really think about the words you write and the effect they may have on those who read them.

Beyond writing itself, what else can you do to make the world a better place for writers and readers? What can you do now to make your future and the future of others brighter? Here are some possibilities:

Literacy Programs

If you're a writer, you will always want people to be able to read your work. There are many adults and children, though, who are not able to make sense of the written word. There may be people in your community who are from a different country and cannot yet read or write English.

Literacy organizations help people to learn basic reading skills. They may need young writers like you to provide tutoring services or to help out with fund raising efforts. If you're interested in helping others learn to read, look up "literacy" in your phone book and give them a call. They may have a special volunteer program for kids your age.

Read Aloud

Nursing homes, homeless shelters, and organizations that serve the blind and disabled are always looking for people to read to their residents or clients. They may need people to read specific publications—like the newspaper, for instance—or they may be excited about having a writer, like you, read a work in progress. Either way, you've helped bring the written word to someone who may not have had the opportunity to discover this world on their own. And you may even have a chance to get some valuable feedback on your own work.

This might be a terrific opportunity for your writer's group, for your church youth organization, or for another service agency that you are involved with.

For more information on programs like these, call your local homeless foundation, the state department of rehabilatative services, or local senior citizens organizations. Be sure to ask for the help of an adult—your parents, your church group advisor, your scout leader, for instance—in organizing this kind of project.

Literary or Cultural Centers

There may also be a not-for-profit literary or cultural center in your community that offers writing classes or supports writers. Give them a call and see if there are any volunteer opportunities there. Perhaps you can give tours, help with fund raisers, or participate in special events.

Libraries

One of the best ways to get to know books is to spend a lot of time with them! Volunteering at your library is a great way to do just that. Your school or local library may need people to shelve books or perform other clerical tasks. They may also need people to help out with special events like story time. Once again, you may have the opportunity to get feedback on your work from a very specific audience. Your school librarian, youth services librarian, or local "friends of the library" group might have some other ideas about ways you can get involved.

WRITE, WRITE, WRITE

As a young writer, you know how to express your opinions through the written word. Now put your writing to work! Write letters to your congressperson about how you feel about political issues, especially political issues that affect you and your writing. How will proposed budget cuts affect funding for writers? What about cuts to education? Let them know what you think!

If you don't like something that's going on in your school, write to your school board or your superintendent. If you think that young writers need to be taken more seriously in your community, write to your local writer's groups and let them know that you are out there!

Taking yourself seriously as a writer means taking your role as a writer and a citizen of the world seriously as well. By taking a stand, getting involved, or working to help others, you're helping to create your own future, a future in which reading and writing are valued activities.

YOUR FUTURE CAREER

When I was a young writer, I was terribly discouraged about my ability to make a living writing. Many of the adults I cared about took my writing seriously, but suggested that I would never be able to make living doing it. I better have a back-up, they said, some kind of job that would support my writing career.

When I entered the real world of employment, I proved them wrong! I've been able to make a career of writing and to support my family. And I've enjoyed every minute of it.

You may have had adults tell you the same thing. Don't believe it! There are plenty of career opportunities for writers. Just take a look around you. The written word is everywhere. Someone is paid to produce all those printed materials. And, although you're probably too young to start charting your career path now, you might want to get to know some of the people in your community who are involved in writing professionally.

Newspapers, magazines, newsletters, and other kinds of publishing companies have staffs of professional wordsmiths that may include writers, copy editors, proofreaders, typesetters, and marketers. All of these people are involved in putting together the publications the company produces. They all have specific jobs, but they are all involved in writing and creating the best publications possible.

If you've ever followed a set of written instructions, you've probably read the work of a technical writer. A technical writer's job is to translate technical information into language that the reader can understand. Companies that produce computer software, high-tech machinery, or other services that need technical support (like your phone or electrical company, for instance) all have technical writers on staff. Their jobs may involve writing manuals or other materials that explain how machinery is operated, how equipment is assembled, how computer programs work, or what steps need to be taken to make a service operational.

Any business that sells a product has to get information about that product into the hands of their customers. Most businesses use written materials—catalogs, brochures, advertisements—to inform the public about the benefits of their product. They may also advertise on television, on the radio, or produce videos to bring customers in. The person who writes all of this material is called a copywriter. Copywriters have some special challenges. They are often limited by space, time, and money. Most copywriters have to master the art of twisting a phrase just right to get a customer's attention. This means that a copywriter has to have a special command of language.

Most companies also need public relations specialists to get the word out about what the company does. Public relations specialists spread the "good news" about a company. They may write about how the company is doing things in the community, what kinds of staff they have and products they produce, and why their role is important in society. Public relations specialists also respond to crises, disasters, or negative publicity. Often, public relations writers produce brochures, financial reports, newspaper articles, and other written materials that support the company's business efforts.

Many public agencies and not-for-profit groups also need public relations writers on staff to write about their efforts in the community. Again, these writers often put their message in the form of a brochure, a report, or a feature story for a magazine or newspaper.

And beyond these professional wordsmiths who work in offices or corporate complexes, there are many writers and editors who work for "hire," who take on various projects on a free-lance basis. These writers usually enjoy being their own boss and making their own choices about how they spend their time. They are often able to complete some of their more creative writing projects because they are supporting their efforts with freelance work.

FINDING OUT MORE

If you are already thinking ahead to your career, there are several ways that you can find out more about these opportunities.

Most writers and professional editors are happy to talk about their career, their background, and what they do on a daily basis. You might try writing them a letter and asking them to tell you a bit about what their work is like, what parts they enjoy, and what problems they encounter.

You might also contact a local publishing company or newspaper and set up an appointment with one of their staff members. Make sure that you keep the time you spend short and focused. Ask for no more than a half an hour and be very direct about what you want to find out. After you've completed your "interview," write a thank you note to the individual expressing your appreciation for the time they spent with you.

"Shadowing" a writing professional is another way to learn more about what that person does. Shadowing a person usually means following them around for an entire day. (Many schools have shadowing programs as part of their ongoing career education.) If you do arrange to shadow a professional in the writing field, be clear about what you want to learn, and don't expect the editor or writer to devote his or her entire attention to you. They have a certain amount of business they need to get done, too. Your role is to observe them going about their business.

Don't hesitate to pitch in and help, if you feel it's appropriate. Offer to make copies, file, or take on any other tasks that you might feel will lighten their load and teach you more about what they do.

Finally, for older writers, those in high school or in college primarily, some companies offer publishing internships. Internships actually allow you first-hand experience with a publishing company. They may be paid or unpaid. You may also arrange to do an internship as part of an independent study through your school.

You can learn more about internships at your local library or through your school's counselor. You can also call publishing companies or other agencies and ask if they offer the internships. If they don't have an existing program, perhaps they would consider starting a new one for young writer like you.

KEEP ON WRITING—SOME FINAL THOUGHTS

Some serious writers seek to publish their work, but publishing certainly isn't the only reason to write. Serious writers write to express themselves, to give voice to some personal issues, or to help them work out a problem.

Serious writers write because they *have* to.

Whether you publish your work or not, or whether you ultimately end up with a career in writing or in some other field, what you are doing is important, meaningful, and powerful. Don't ever stop doing it. Don't ever let anyone tell you that it's not important or that you won't make money doing it or that it's a waste of time. Don't ever stop working at your craft.

Don't ever stop saying, I AM A WRITER.

It's what makes you the special person you are.

PUBLISHING POETRY
by Jennifer Bosveld

TIPS TO MAKE SURE YOU'RE READY!

Before you investigate who might publish your poetry, save postage and time and take another look at your poem. Your own love of it may help you in revising it. Revise, re-vise [re-see] it again. But first let's identify some ways to make better poems earlier in the process.

Occasionally, something happens during the day that produces an emotional response in us. When that happens, some of us are driven to write a poem. Maybe we feel great loss because a friend moved out of state or we are excited that school's out for the summer and the new swimming pool is waiting. *Warning:* Important life experiences can lead to dreadful poetry. If you're not saying some brand new thing about a situation like this, chances are, you're not getting to the poetry; however, any writing is worthwhile, it keeps your hand moving across the page, keeps you mentally and physically limber for writing when those original thoughts do come.

CREATING "FELT EXPERIENCE." TAKE A PICTURE OF A MOMENT!

Capture the moment, perhaps even a specific five minutes, in a way that gives your reader "felt experience". An exercise I developed as a poet in the schools is called "Taking A Picture Of The Moment." In your mind's eye, snap a picture of a particular place. Try a corner of your classroom. If this were an actual picture, tiny objects would come into focus before your eyes. Pretend the page is the film, words are the chemicals that mix and slide into vivid pictorial relationships. Bring the objects into focus in your poem. Provide precise details, the actual material objects, and the action verbs that best portray the motion, the change, and the relationships in that picture.

Place in your poem physical objects that create sensations, that let us *experience* rather than be told "about" your experience. Give us the stuff of your life; things in boxes in your closet, anything noisy, something that stinks, something broken, something you want out of the house, or something that feels like a celebration unto itself every time you look upon it.

After you've written a poem, you might try asking yourself the strangest questions you can imagine about what you've written so far. For example, if you are writing a poem about a walk home from school, how could you make that as captivating as possible? Even though an actual event might have inspired you, be willing to create fresh relationships and challenging complications for the sake of the story or poem. Try this: without thinking about the poem at all, simply make a list of nine unrelated specific objects. I'll make one here:

screwdriver	semi tire against a chainlink fence
green lampshade	purple airplane
pig	full gallon of chocolate milk
peach pie	paring knife
garbage can rolling down the street	

The word artist often leaves the old reality to invent a new reality on the page. Try to force each of these nine items into the poem. Perhaps most of them won't work and you'll take them out. But some probably will make all the difference toward getting the reader's interest.

Identify objects down to their most specific name. Did you call that thing in the driveway a "car" or did you mention the car's name? Would it make the poem more interesting to become more specific?

Don't let FORM boss your poem around. If you have a tendency to rhyme, force yourself not to. Choose words because they lend clarity and interest to the poem, not because they rhyme.

PUBLISHING YOUR POETRY

After you've gotten twenty or thirty poems written and revised, you might want to see them in print. Do NOT fall for those publishers who advertise contests and end up asking for $47 for a copy of the book they're squeezing your poem into with a bunch of others on the page. If your poem was good enough to help make a book worth buying and reading, a respectable publisher would want to pay you for the poem by giving you at least a free copy of the book. Avoid contests that advertise in the backs of slick magazines and that come out with news releases several times a year about their so-called competitions. Know who you're sending poetry to. Often parents, librarians, and teachers do not know the scams from the legitimate opportunities for you. You can call the literary coordinator at your local state arts council if you want to know if a publisher tends to be trusted. Many of these coordinators are extremely knowledgeable about publishing opportunities for young poets.

START YOUR OWN LITTLE PRESS

It might be fun to invent your own publishing company for your poetry and your friends'. It could provide you with valuable experience that helps you become a major publisher as an adult. You could try to negotiate with a small press publisher in your area for two hours of their time. You might be able to barter your time to help out with their work in exchange for their help with yours! Possibly, if a student volunteered an afternoon of collating, cleaning book shelves, and licking envelopes, I'd give that student a free lesson on starting a kids' press, just because I'd like to see it happen in my community and yours.

SUBMITTING POETRY TO EDITORS OF MAGAZINES

Make this last minute check. Place your poem next to the magazine you're sending it to. Take another look at the poems the editors have chosen. Does yours really seem to fit in? If you think it might, go ahead and give it a try.

Send three poems on 20-lb white paper, a cover note that gives your age, grade, school, and interests, and try to type all this or produce it on a computer. Some publishers, depending on the project, might prefer getting something in your own handwriting. Find out what they want before you prepare the submission. Send a self-addressed stamped envelope (SASE) for their writer's guidelines.

Make sure your name and complete address appear in the upper left hand corner of each poem, give each poem its own page, and enclose a SASE. Be prepared to wait many weeks, maybe months for an answer. Keep a record of what poem you send where, honoring each poem with its own manila folder, title of poem at the top, and on the front, this simple record:

1/16/96 Cricket Magazine _____

If you get back a note that says they're sorry they can't use the poem, add in the third column the word "sorry" and the date you got the "sorry". Train yourself not to care when a note comes back that they can't use the poem. Pouting is not part of the procedure. Here's what you do instead:

1. Take a fresh look at the poem. Go through all the critiquing processes. Revise the poem if it can stand it.
2. Send it out again. Right Away.
3. Or, decide that publishing isn't all that important to you right now; writing better poetry is.

CLASSROOM PUBLISHING PROJECTS

It is quite common today for classrooms and school writing programs to publish their own school literary magazines. The work and voices we hear in them are exciting opportunities for everyone involved. Perhaps a local business would sponsor the project. Start out simple. You can create a volume of 48 pages or so for very little money. There is probably knowledgable help in your area for starting a project like this. Sometimes these arenas provide the exposure for helping companies like Raspberry Publications discover new talent!

Jennifer Bosveld is director of *Pudding House Writers' Resource Center,* 60 N. Main St., Johnstown, Ohio 43031, and of the *Young Writers' Workshop / Playshop.* She has been a poet in the schools and in human services for fifteen years and is widely published, appearing in over 400 literary journals. Send SASE for information about any Pudding House opportunites for your writers.

ON WRITING PLAYS
by Laura Hembree

So, you have chosen to be a writer! To tell stories, to express ideas and even, perhaps ,to write a play! By that choice, you can participate in the most ancient tradition of passing knowledge directly from person to person, face to face; for plays, unlike any other form of writing, are meant to be performed. Plays are as old as humanity itself and as new as the freshest idea that you, the playwright, commits to paper.

THE WRITER
First, you must write, everyday. Even if you write for just ten minutes, do it everyday. It does not matter what you write. Write anything! If nothing comes to mind, write about the sounds coming through the window, the drops of moisture forming on the side of your can of soda, write about your teachers, or your fellow students. To a writer everything is interesting. Nothing you perceive or think is insignificant. NOTHING!

Second, writers must observe. See the world around you; the sky, the sofa, the sidewalk, strangers, your family, yourself. The world and the people in the world coupled with the ideas in your head are the writer's raw material. Unlike the painter or the sculptor who must buy his paints or clay, your observations cost nothing and can be done anytime, anywhere.

Third, in the early stages of writing a story or a play do not edit yourself. Do not try to judge your own work, just write. The early moments of any creative work must unfold without censorship, especially your own.

Fourth, trust yourself!! That may be the most important idea of all and the most difficult to hang on to. Your instincts and perceptions may not be what others see and feel, and it is too easy to dismiss the validity of your own experiences. Do not dismiss your own instincts, on the contrary, anchor yourself in them. By relying on your perceptions, observations and instincts you will sharpen them, deepen them, and offer something unique and valuable in your writing.

THE STORY

At the center of every story is a conflict that the characters seek to resolve. *How* they seek to resolve the conflict is what makes the story interesting, funny or tragic. The conflict need not be earthshaking. In fact, it is often the small conflicts in our lives which can be the most interesting.

What, exactly, is a conflict? Think about a person standing in front of a mirror trying to decide how he should comb his hair. That is a conflict. A minor conflict, perhaps, but one that is tied to every other aspect of his personality *and* the situation in which he finds himself. Why is he so concerned about his hair? Is he worried about what his friends think? Is today the terrifying day he has decided to speak to the new girl in homeroom? This is a conflict around which an entire story could be written. For instance:

Maybe our character seeks to resolve the conflict by combing his hair in a way that makes him look like a certain rock star. Then he begins to walk and act like this rock star. When he introduces himself to the new girl in homeroom, however, his behavior is so pretentious she brushes him off. This simple conflict and resolution about his hair not only propels us into the story, it also reveals to us the character's personality, his wants, his values and his insecurities while also telling us about the girl he is trying to impress. This is a simple conflict and resolution.

THE PLAY

What makes a play different than a novel or short story?

Plays *show* stories rather than tell them. They are not simply read, plays are *seen and heard*. There are three tools the playwright uses to create a good play:

Dialogue, Movement, and Space

Dialogue

How a person talks, how she phrases her words, how she pauses, or plunges ahead all tell you as much about her as the actual content of her speech.

Dialogue is not made up of only words, but rhythms,

phrases, pauses and plunges. As a playwright, it is important that you silence yourself in order to listen to others. Those others include the real people around you and the characters you have created.

When you listen to the people around you or your characters' voices, *hear* their natural rhythms of speech. Be aware of the words and speech patterns used by different age groups. Pay attention to how men and women use words differently. *Do not put your own words into your characters' mouths* or else you will have dialogue that is untruthful and unconvincing. Let your characters put their words into your pen and on your page. Your characters are very wise, even when they are foolish.

Movement

Pretend that you are walking into a room. Inside you see three members of your family. One is crouched near another who is crying, the third is standing, staring angrily at the other two. There is broken glass on the floor and within seconds, without a word being spoken, you understand what has happened. The angry person is clenching and unclenching both fists, while verbally denying any feeling of anger. The crying person is turned away from the angry one, seemingly emotionally hurt but speaking words that make the angry person feel guilty. The person between them is nervously moving back and forth between the other two. You observe that the words being said by each of the characters do not agree with their body language, their movement or the tone of their voice.

A playwright knows that words alone do not necessarily tell the truth about the situation or about the people within it; in fact, words are often used to hide the truth.

How a person moves, when a person pauses or is silent may reveal more than words. A person bites his nails, another fiddles with her skirt, another keeps slapping other people on the back and smiling. These are gestures that reveal the character's state of mind, which the character may be desperately trying to hide with words.

For instance;

Two men are talking, one stands looking at himself in the

mirror. The conversation is about business or football, but how the man looks at himself in the mirror, what he does while looking in the mirror will reveal things to the audience they would never learn from the conversation between the men. Although the playwright does not dictate exactly how the actor will choose to portray the character, he does need to be aware that plays are physical, and physical choices, such as a man looking into a mirror, are invaluable. In an instant you have exposed an aspect of your character to the audience which may have been inadequately expressed in words alone.

Space

Let us again walk into that room with the three family members and the broken glass. Is the space a cramped bedroom at home or is it an empty locker room at school? Each setting has a very different feel. Behavior which is acceptable in the locker room might be inappropriate at home. Everyone in your audience instinctively understands that different settings create different demands on behavior.

The setting is a kind of character. Settings have personalities. Compare how different the living room feels from the attic or the difference between a friend's bedroom and your own. Think about what makes these rooms distinct. Is it their size, their function or the objects within them? The role your setting plays is as important as the role of your characters.

All things are worthy of being examined by a writer. Anchor yourself in yourself, observe, and write.

Laura Hembree lives in New York City where she has worked as a researcher, cab driver, waitress, community organizer, dancer and choreographer. Her play *Carpool* , examines the condition of the American middle class man at the end of the 20th century. *Carpool* received it's world premiere at the Detroit Repertory Theater.

BOOK PUBLISHERS

PLAGIARISM

Webster's New World Dictionary says *plagiarism* is passing off the work of another as your own. It also defines *stealing* as the taking of another's property without permission. Plagiarism is simply stealing, but it is more than passing off another person's work as your own.

When you pretend that the words you write are yours, everyone loses. The real author loses because the credit for his or her efforts has gone to the wrong person. The audience you lied to will lose faith in you and will never look at your work the same way again. But, most importantly, you lose.

You have lost your self-respect; you have lost the thrill of creating something special of your own; you have lost the unique feeling of accomplishment that comes from creating something special.

Stealing is a losing proposition for everyone. So be honest. You will feel better, and in the process of creating, you will learn more about the craft of being a writer.

After all, if a company does publish your stolen work, you will know that it isn't yours and you will have lost the joy of being a real author. And your readers will have missed something of great value—**you!**

FREE SPIRIT PUBLISHING, INC.
400 First Ave. N., Suite 616
Minneapolis, MN 55401-1730   ages: 14 and up

First book by a young person (17 years old) was published in 1993. Specializes in SELF HELP FOR KIDS. Main interests include the development of self-esteem, self awareness, creative thinking and problem solving abilities, assertiveness, and making a difference in the world. Children have a lot to share with each other. They also can reach and teach each other in ways adults cannot.

Submission Information:
"We accept submissions from young people ages 14 and older. Please request a catalog and writer's guidelines before submitting manuscripts (specify student guidelines). Publishes psychology, self-help, how-to, and education. Pays advance and royalties. Submit manuscripts to M.E. Salzmann, editorial assistant. Send query. Will accept typewritten manuscripts. SASE. Reports in 3-4 months.

KOPPER BEAR PRESS
P.O. Box 19454
Boulder, CO 80308-2454   ages: 13-21

May also reach via CompuServe: Howard S. Bashinski 70732,2505. New book publisher dedicated to helping exceptional authors between ages 13-21 get published in high-quality format. Publishes fiction, non-fiction, poetry, short stories, novels, novellas, essays, etc., from young people ages 13-21. Is very interested in publishing novels written by young people.

Submission Information:
Will accept typed or handwritten work, but be sure you keep a copy as submissions are not returned. For additional information e-mail to the above CompuServe number.

LANDMARK EDITIONS, INC.
1402 Kansas Ave.
Kansas City, MO 64127
(see contest listing)   ages: 6-19
NATIONAL WRITTEN & ILLUSTRATED BY . . .
AWARDS CONTEST FOR STUDENTS

RAINTREE/STECK-VAUGHN PUBLISHERS
P.O. Box 27010
Austin, TX 78755
(see contest listing)   grades: 4-6
PUBLISH-A-BOOK CONTEST

RASPBERRY PUBLICATIONS, INC.
P.O. Box 925
Westerville, OH 43086-6925   grades: K-12
(800) 759-7171
Fax: (614) 899-6147

This is a publishing company created to showcase the writing
talents of children and students, K-12th grades. "We believe
that not only do young authors deserve a chance for early
recognition, but that their works provide a valuable learning
experience for other children to share." Accepts manuscripts
throughout the year. Prefers works written and illustrated by
the same author, but will accept joint efforts. All subjects are
considered including fiction and non-fiction. A new series of
books, *The Raspberry Crime Files,* always needs good mysteries, but other topics of interest include fantasy, romance, and
real-life events that reflect your lives, families, schools and
friends. Also looking for books written about learning math
from a child's point of view and would like to see *"101 Favorite
Science Experiments Kids Can Do"* (Nothing explosive that
might blow up your house or rearrange your bedroom) Whatever your passion in life is, write about it. Require a signed
statement of originality and contract defining rights by parents, guardian, teacher or librarian.

Submission Information:
Submit copy of previously unpublished manuscript and illustrations (not all books require illustrations). Picture books must contain a minimum of 16 pages. Nonpicture books must contain a minimum of 64 pages (you may submit more than one story to reach this minimum, but they must all be within the same genre. All mysteries, or romances etc.) Will accept typed, legibly handwritten or computer printout manuscripts. Neatness and overall presentation counts. Ask for a copy of the rules and guidelines for submitting manuscripts. Submit text and illustrations to Curt Jenkins or Susan Schmidt, publishers. Pays royalties but not advances. Reports within 2-4 months.

TYKETOON YOUNG AUTHORS PUBLISHING COMPANY
7417 Douglas Lane
Fort Worth, TX 76180   grades: 1-8

Publishes fiction, non-fiction, and poetry picture books written and illustrated by students in first through eighth grades; publishes one book or more from each grade level. Our audience is same age students, teachers, parents, and other interested readers of all ages. Authors are expected to write for the interest level of their own age audience and not to "write down". The purpose in publishing works by young authors: To provide "real life" incentives to write; to publish models of good youthauthored writing, and to use the published books as teaching tools modeling excellent writing.

Submission Information:
The search is ongoing; manuscripts are accepted throughout the year. Authors and illustrators may collaborate; books are judged in the grade level of the highest grade collaborator. Books will be from 16 to 32 pages in length (no word-count limits). Will accept legible handwritten or typewritten manuscripts. Illustrations must accompany every manuscript. Use of guidelines is encouraged; guidelines available by request only when a SASE is enclosed with the submission. Submit manuscripts to Tyketoon Young Author-Illustrator Search. Reports in 3 months.

MAGAZINE PUBLISHERS

COPYRIGHT . . . OR WHO OWNS WHAT?

Copyright laws protect creators of original works. They give you, the author or artist, the sole right to reproduce, sell, or distribute your work. Owning the copyright means that you have the power to *decide how and by whom* your work will be used.

Any work you have created is automatically protected by law. That law protects all original material including photographs, illustrations, electronic recordings and written material. It is not necessary to file a formal copyright registration to protect your work. If a publisher wants to use your material, it is the publisher's responsibility to register that material with the copyright office.

There are many different ways a publisher will "buy" your material. For example, a magazine may want the *First North American Serial Rights* which gives them permission to publish material in their periodical before it appears in book form. After that, the rights revert back to you or the copyright holder. (See other examples of rights in the glossary.)

A book publisher might buy *All Rights* which means that they own that property, it is no longer yours, but you will receive authorship credit. Many contests assume all rights to your work once it has been submitted whether that work is published or not. Be careful. Your rights are all that you are being paid for.

Many publishers require adults to sign publishing contracts in addition to the authors. Publishers will define contract and copyright policies in their rules and guidelines. Read them carefully. Copyrights and contracts can be confusing and complicated, so be sure you understand them **BEFORE** you sign anything.

For more information and a free Copyright Information Kit, contact:

Copyright Office
Library of Congress
Washington, D.C. 20559
(202) 707-9100

THE APPRENTICE WRITER

c/o Gary Fincke
Susquehanna University
Selinsgrove, PA 17870   grades: 9-12

Magazine published annually. "Writing by high school students and for high school students." Purpose in publishing
works by young people: To provide quality writing by students
which can be read for pleasure and serve as a text for high
school classrooms. Work is primarily from the eastern and
northeastern states, but will consider work from other areas of
U.S. Students must be in grades 9-12. Writer's guidelines
available with SASE.

Submission Information:

Uses 15 short stories (prefers under 5,000 words); 15 nonfiction personal essays (prefers under 5,000 words); 60 poems (no
word limit) per issue. Pays in copies to writers and their
schools. Submit complete manuscripts to Gary Fincke, editor.
Will accept typewritten work. SASE. Submit manuscripts by
March 15. Responds by May of each year.

BOODLE: BY KIDS, FOR KIDS

P.O. Box 1049
Portland, IN 47371   ages: 6-12

Audience: Children 6-12. Publishes student-produced stories,
articles, poems, mazes and puzzles. Readers are invited to
write and illustrate their own ideas and send them to the
editors. Uses about twelve short stories and twenty to thirty
poems per issue. Seldom publishes sad or depressing stories
about death or serious illness. Especially likes humor and
offbeat stories and poems. Never devotes more than two pages
to any one story, so long stories are not acceptable. Handwritten material OK, if legible. Please include full name, address,
grade when written, current grade, name of school, and a
statement from parent or teacher that the work is original.
Send SASE for reply, or if you wish your material returned.
Guidelines available with SASE. Sample copies $2.50. Pay-
ment is two free copies of issue. Reports in two months.

Submission Information:
Young writers and artists should read BOODLE to see what kind of material is published. Try to think of something different than the stories you read. What kind of story would you like to read? The best way to get your story or poem published is to make the editor smile or laugh when she reads it.

CHICKADEE MAGAZINE
179 John Street, Suite 500
Toronto, Ontario M5T 3G5, Canada   ages: 3-8

Science and nature magazine for ages 3-8 published ten times a year. Publishes readers' artwork and writing in response to requests in the "Chirp" section of the magazine. Publishes drawings on a specific topic, a letter with photo from readers, and a "chuckle" submitted by a child. Very occasionally, publishes short poems by readers in "Chirp".
Submission Information:
All materials submitted to "Chirp" become the property of Owl Communications. No payment made for submissions.

CHILD LIFE
1100 Waterway Blvd.
P.O. Box 567
Indianapolis, IN 46206   ages: 9-11

Publication for children 9-11 from the Children's Better Health Institute. Stresses health-related themes or ideas including nutrition, safety, exercise and proper health habits. Publishes from readers: Original fiction, nonfiction and poetry, favorite jokes and riddles.
Submission Information:
Submissions do not have to be health related. Tries to publish one original story (up to 400 words) in each issue. Please write your name, age, school, complete address and home phone number on each submission. Jokes and riddles can be sent on

postcards. Material cannot be returned. No payment for published reader material. Send SASE for special guidelines for young writers. Sample copy $1.25. Usually selects materal sent by children in the 9-11 age group.

CHILDREN'S DIGEST
1100 Waterway Blvd.
P.O. Box 567
Indianapolis, IN 46206   ages: Pre-teens

Publication for preteens from the Children's Better Health Institute. Stresses health-related themes or ideas including nutrition, safety, exercise and proper health habits. Publishes from readers: Original fiction, nonfiction and poetry, favorite jokes and riddles. Material need not be health-related. Stories printed occasionally.

Submission Information:
If possible, please type stories. Put your name, age, school and complete address on each page. Fiction and nonfiction stories may be up to 300 words. Material cannot be returned. Jokes and riddles can be sent on postcards. No payment for published reader material. Send SASE for special guidelines for young writers. Sample copies $1.25

CHILDREN'S PLAYMATE
1100 Waterway Blvd.
P.O. Box 567
Indianapolis, IN 46206   ages: 6-8

Publication for children 6-8 from the Children's Better Health Institute. Stresses health-related themes or ideas including nutrition, safety, exercise and proper health habits.

Submission Information:
Poetry must be original. Artwork must be drawn by the reader. Jokes and riddles can be favorite ones readers have heard. Jokes and riddles can be sent on postcards. Sorry, no material

can be returned. No payment for published reader material.
Send SASE for guidelines. Sample copies $1.25. Submissions
limited to young people ages 6-8.

CREATIVE KIDS
Prufrock Press
P.O. Box 8813
Waco, TX 76714-8813   ages: 8-14

Kids from all over the nation contribute to the largest magazine written by and for kids.
Publishes: Stories, games, puzzles, poetry, artwork, opinion,
and photography by and for kids ages 8-14. Work must be
original and submitted by the author. Work submitted to
Creative Kids should not be under consideration by any other
publisher.
Submission Information:
Each submission must be labeled with the child's name,
birthday, grade, school and home address, and must include a
cover letter. All submissions must include SASE for reply. For
detailed guidelines, send SASE. Sample copy $3.00.
Editor's Remarks: *"Creative Kids, The National Voice for
Kids,* bursts with new ideas and activities to entertain, excite
and encourage the creativity of kids ages 8-14. The magazine
includes exciting examples of the most creative student work
to be found in any publication for kids."
Subscription Rates: One-year (6 issues) $19.95

CREATIVE WITH WORDS
P.O. Box 223226
Carmel, CA 93922   ages: 7-19

Publishes one anthology per month, many for or by children.
Publishes folk/artistic tales and such; creative writing by
children (poetry, prose and language art); creative writing in
special-interest groups (senior citizens, handicapped, general

family). Particularly interested in prose, language arts work, fillers, puzzles and poems from young people.

Submission Information:
Submissions from young writers must be their own work and not edited, corrected or rewritten by an adult. Will work with individual young writers if editing and corrections are necessary. Do not send personal photo unless requested. Use standard format for preparing manuscripts. Poetry must be 20 lines or less. Prose should not exceed 1,000 words. Shorter poems and articles always welcome. Do not send previously published material. Copyright reverts to author after publication. No payment is made to contributors, but they do receive a 20 percent cost reduction on publication in which their work appears. No free copies in payment. SASE must accompany all correspondence and manuscripts. Send SASE for current guidelines. Address submisions to B. Geltrich.

Note: Please check the contest section for current themes for Creative With Words Publications.

HIGHLIGHTS FOR CHILDREN
803 Church Street
Honesdale, PA 18431   ages: 2-12

Published monthly for youngsters ages 2-12. Publishes poems, drawings and stories from readers. Also runs two unfinished stories a year, to which readers submit their creative endings. For writers 16 or older, also reviews submissions of short stories, factual features, puzzles, party plans, crafts, finger plays and action plays. Seldom buys verse.

Submission Information:
For writers up to age 15, drawings may be in color or black-and-white. Prose may be no more than two double-spaced hand-written pages. Acknowledges all material submitted. However, material is not returned; do not enclose SASE. No payment made for contributions from writers 15 or under. For writers 16 and older, consult regular free-lance guidelines; available free. Fiction should not be more than 800 words; pays $.08 and up

per word. Science and factual articles within 800 words bring
$75 and up. Other material brings $25 and up. Those 16 and
older should send complete manuscript with SASE. All submissions need to include name, age and complete home address. Personal photo not necessary.

HOW ON EARTH!
P.O. Box 339
Oxford, PA 19363   ages: 13-24

HOE! is a nonprofit, all volunteer quarterly magazine for and
by teenagers concerned about environmental, animal and
global issues. Celebrates and provides a voice for young people's creativity, passion and concern for all life. HOE! encour-
ages young people to feel and think for themselves and is a
celebration of every person's potential to make a difference.
HOE! is geared toward youth ages 13-24. Youth are also
involved in all aspects of planning, development and production. Publishes research articles, poetry, creative writing and
essays concerning ecology, ethics, animal, global and social
issues, health, vegetarianism, vegetarian lifestyle and activ-
ism. Original artwork and photographs accepted. Food articles
and vegetarian recipes suitable for young people encouraged,
as are articles containing practical information for compas-
sionate, ecologically sound living. Authors must be 24 or
younger.
Submission Information:
Include your name, complete address, phone number, and
birth date. Query letter is suggested before submission of
longer articles.
     Submit only material that is consistent with our mission
statement and age guidelines. Include a title for all submissions or indicate that it should remain untitled. A completed
HOE! Questionnaire must either be on file at the HOE! office
or accompanying your submission. Contact our office for a copy
of the questionnaire. Submit only original writing, poetry, art
work or photographs. Indicate whether recipes are original,

from a cookbook, or adapted from a cookbook. All recipes and food reviews must be pure vegetarian. Send a SASE for complete guidelines. Sample copy $6.00. Welcomes ideas, input and participation from its readers in every way possible.

HUMPTY DUMPTY'S MAGAZINE
1100 Waterway Blvd.
P.O. Box 567
Indianapolis, IN 46206   ages: 4-6

Publication for children 4-6 from the Children's Better Health Institute. Stresses health-related themes or ideas including nutrition, safety, exercise and proper habits. Publishes from readers: Kidtalk (responses from readers on various topics - see the magazine) and You Draw the Pictures (original art).
Submission Information:
Please write your name, age, and complete address on each submission. Material cannot be returned. No payment for published reader material. Send SASE for special guidelines for young writers. Sample copies $1.25. Selects material sent by children in the 4-6 age group.

INK BLOT
Margaret Larkin, editor
Vicki Larkin, assistant editor
901 Day Road
Saginaw, MI 48609   ages: 5-19

Monthly newsletter designed to provide a new outlet for young writers and artists. Distributed to local schools, libraries and hospital waiting rooms. Publishes fiction and nonfiction essays, short stories, poetry, and acrostics. Will consider other short manuscripts and black-and-white (2" x 3") artwork. Especially in need of short fillers. No photos.
Submission Information:
Handwritten is accepted; typed material preferred. Students

should include name, age, grade and school name. Short fillers should be 25-75 words long. Poetry limited to 30 lines. Maximum length for essays and stories is 500 words (must fit on one page). No submissions returned, however, contributors retain copyright. If you send SASE, you will receive a free copy of the newsletter containing your published work. Guidelines available for SASE. Sample copy $1.00 plus SASE (make check payable to Margaret Larkin, editor). Likes to receive material written from your heart. Remember to send your best work. Double-check for grammar, spelling and writing errors before mailing. We want to promote a positive outlook to our readers. We do not want negative or derogatory material.

JACK AND JILL
1100 Waterway Blvd.
P.O. Box 567
Indianapolis, IN 46206   ages: 7-10

Publication for children 7-10 from the Children's Better Health Institute. Stresses health-related themes or ideas including nutrition, safety, exercise and proper health habits. Publishes original poetry, favorite jokes and riddles from readers. Occasionally publishes original stories (500 words or less) and original drawings.
Submission Information:
Submissions do not have to be health-related. Please write your name, age, school and complete address on each submission. Jokes and riddles can be sent on postcards. Material cannot be returned. No payment for published reader material. Send SASE for guidelines for young writers. Sample copies $1.25. Selects material sent in by children in the 7-10 age group.

KID'S KORNER NEWSLETTER
P.O. Box 413
Joaquin, TX 75954   ages: 6-17

Newsletter written for kids and by kids under age 18. Marcella Simmons, editor. Publishes fiction and nonfiction written by kids, for kids under age 18. Also artwork on any theme.
Submission Information:
Handwritten material accepted. Manuscript length for fiction 100-2,000 words; for nonfiction 50-500 words. Sample copy $1.00. Double-check for grammar, spelling and writing errors before mailing.

KIDS N'SIBS
191 Whittier Road
Rochester, NY 14624   ages: 6-21
e-mail: dhcy@uhura.cc.rochester.edu

Elizabeth Fogg, editor. Free newsletter focusing on sharing the views and experiences of disabled children and siblings. Publishes anything as long as it's in good taste and relates to newsletter's theme. Prefers submissions made by those 21 and under, but will publish stories by older writers if they are personal accounts of their childhoods and what it was like as a disabled child or sibling of one. Also interested in information on different disabilities and diseases.
Submission Information:
Submissions longer than one column or page will be used, with author's permission, as a series. No guidelines available. May contact by regular or e-mail. Send SASE for free sample. No payment. Contributors receive free copy with published piece. This newsletter is for anyone with an interest in disabilities and handicaps. Feel free to write to us or just subscribe. Currently there aren't any rewards for submitting an article because there isn't any charge for subscription.

LISTEN MAGAZINE
Lincoln Steed, editor
55 WestOak Ridge Drive
Haggerstown, MD 21740   ages: 13-19

A monthly publication for teens and young adults, encouraging
the development of good habits and high ideals of physical and
mental health. Paticularly aims to educate positively against
alcohol and other drug use. Publishes special column for teens
called "Listening", using short, well-written, thought-provok-
ing poems, stories and essays from teen writers in each issue.
Also factual features or opinion essays with or without accompanying quality photos, narratives based on true-life inci-
dents, poetry, puzzles and cartoons.
Submission Information:
Submissions for "Listening" should include age, grade, school,
etc.; no photos. Poetry limited to 20 lines; stories and essays
300-500 words. Adress to "Listening" in care of LISTEN MAG-
AZINE. Include SASE. Send for free writer's guidelines and tip
sheet. Samples available for $1.00 and large manila envelope
with SASE. No payment for "Listening", but contributors will
receive a free LISTEN T-shirt. Other material rates between
$.05-.10 per word.

MERLYN'S PEN: THE NATIONAL
MAGAZINES OF STUDENT WRITING,
P.O. Box 1058
East Greenwich, RI 02818-0964   Grades: 6-12

Two magazines, Intermediate and Senior High Editions, written by students in grades 6-12. Four issues per year. Publishes
stories, plays, poems, essays on important issues, review
letters, word games, opinions, critiques of writing in magazine,
and art by students in grades 6-12. Also considers puzzles.
Letters to the editor welcome. Available in bookstores and by
subscription. Call 1-800-247-2027 for information.

Submission Information:

Authors and artists receive three complimentary issues that contain their work. Call or write to request official cover sheet. Submissions received without an official cover sheet will not be reviewed. Response within eleven weeks. Manuscripts must be typed double-spaced with extra-wide margins. No personal photos necessary. Young writers who are successful in "Merlyn's Pen" choose subjects, characters and plots that come from personal experience. For example, they set stories in places they know (school, home, vacation spots, etc.), write about characters their own age, and choose conflicts that they've handled themselves (peer pressure, parents, growing up, sports, etc.). Writing about anything else is bound to be nonspecific, unclear, and therefore unconvincing and unpublishable. More advanced writers can disregard this advice!

OUR LITERATE LEGACY
Bonding Times
P.O. Box 736
Lake Hamilton, FL 33851   ages: 6-18

Bonding Times is a quarterly publication for Christian families. The section "Our Literate Legacy" showcases children's work, opinions, and talents. Publishes most types of written work by children 18 and under; poems, fiction, exegetical reports (interpretations of passages from the Bible), book reviews, field trip reports, letters to the editor, journalism pieces, science project lab reports. Anything that you are already writing for your school subjects or in your personal life will be considered. Artwork also considered.

Submission Information:

All submissions should be typed. Each piece must include name, age, address, school (home, private or public), and signatures of both student and parent stating that work is original and granting *The Bonding Times* permission to publish, market and distribute accepted work per stated compensation. Work becomes the property of The Bonding Times.

Payment is $.02 per word published. Payment for artwork is $1-$10 depending on size, detail and reproducibility. Detailed guidelines and additional information available with SASE. All work must be written from a Christian world view. This is a Christian, pro-family publication.

POETRY CANADA
P.O. Box 106
Kingston, ON K7l 4Y5, Canada   ages: All

Quarterly poetry publication.
Submission Information:
Submit 8-10 poems in standard typed form. Include cover sheet, SASE (or IRCs if submitting from the US). Make sure writer's name appears on every page submitted for publication. Seeks to publish the best poetry in all genres.

SKIPPING STONES:
A MULTICULTURAL CHILDREN'S MAGAZINE
P.O. Box 3939
Eugene, OR 97403-0939   ages: 7-18

Winner of the 1995 Golden Shoestring Award of the Educational Press Association of America.

Skipping Stones is an international, nonprofit, bimonthly children's magazine featuring writing and art by children 7-18. Writing may be submitted in any language and from any country. Publishes original artwork, photos, poems, stories, recipes, songs, games, and book reviews; writings about your background, culture, celebrations, religion, interests and experiences, etc. You may send questions for other readers to "Dear Editor" or "Dear Hanna", to answer or ask for a pen pal. Submissions welcome in all languages (work published in the language submitted, with English translation). Youth Honor Award Program recognizes ten young artists and writers. Submissions for awards by June 25th each year. Themes:

Multicultural and Nature awareness. Entry fees $3.00 entitles you to a copy of the fall issue containing all the winning entries. **Prize:** Certificate, 5 multicultural and/or nature books, subscription to *Skipping Stones*. Theme for 1996: *Envisioning the Life in 2025 A.D.*.

Submission Information:

Prefers original work (keep your own copy). Short pieces preferred. Include your age and a description of your cultural background. Can be typed, handwritten or hand printed. Free copy of the issue in which your work appears. Material not copyrighted for exclusive use. Guidelines available, please enclose SASE or SAE with IRC if possible. Sample copy $5.00. Address submissions, query letters or request for guidelines, themes planned, etc., to: Arun Toke', editor. Subscriptions: $20 per year (5 issues) or $30 for institutions. Airmail or special handling may cost more.

SPRING TIDES

Savannah Country Day Lower School
824 Stillwood Road
Savannah, GA 31419-2643   ages: 5-12

Literary magazine written and illustrated by children ages 5-12. Publishes stories and poems with or without illustrations. Illustrations may be black-and-white or color.

Submission Information:

Any child, ages 5-12, may submit material. Limit stories to 1,200 words and poems to 20 lines. All material must be original and created by the person submitting it. A statement signed by the child's parent or teacher attesting to the originality must accompany all work. Material should be carefully proofread and typed. Each piece must be labeled with the name, birth date, grade, school, home address and school address of the child. Material submitted to *Spring Tides* should not be under consideration by any other publisher. All work must be accompanied by a SASE. Notification of acceptance or rejection will be sent in the SASE. Work not accompanied by a

SASE will be discarded if not used. Students submitting accepted material will receive a copy of the issue in which the work appears. Submit to Connie Huston, editor. Send SASE for guidelines. Sample copy $5.00.

STONE SOUP, THE MAGAZINE BY CHILDREN
Children's Art Foundation
P.O. Box 83
Santa Cruz, CA 95063
1-800-447-4569   ages: 6-13

Each issue includes an activity guide with projects designed to sharpen reading and writing skills. Five issues published yearly. Publishes stories, poems, personal experiences, book reviews and art by children through age 13.
Submission Information:
All submissions must be accompanied by a SASE. Those that are not will not receive a response. Writing need not be typed or copied over. Stories may be any length. Children interested in reviewing books should write the editor, Ms. Gerry Mandel, stating their name, age, address, interests, and the kinds of books they like to read. Children interested in illustrating stories should send two samples of their artwork along with their name, address, age and a description of the kinds of stories they want to illustrate. Reports in four weeks. CAF reserves all rights. Authors of stories and poems receive $10, book reviewers receive $15, and illustrators receive $8 per illustration. All published contributors receive a certificate, plus discounts on subscriptions and single copies. Guidelines available at no charge. Please enclose SASE. Sample copy available for $3.00. Very interested in your experiences. If something that happened to you or something you observed made a strong impression on you, try to turn that experience or observation into a good story or poem. Also look for vivid descriptions of people, places and emotions. Subscription: $24 per year.

TEEN POWER
P.O. Box 632
Glen Ellyn, IL 60138   ages: 11-15

Sunday School take-home paper for young teens ages 11-15;
published quarterly in weekly parts. Publishes true, personal
experience stories of how God has worked in the life of a teen.
Also poetry, nonfiction and puzzles.
Submission Information:
Double-spaced, typed manuscripts only, 500-1,000 words. Always include SASE for return of manuscript or reply. Pays
$.06-.10 per word on acceptance. Reports in eight weeks. Send
business-size envelope (#10) SASE for sample copy and writer's guidelines. Goal is to help teens apply biblical principles
for Christian living to their everyday lives. Everything we
publish must have strong, evangelical Christian basis.

TURTLE MAGAZINE
1100 Waterway Blvd.
P.O. Box 567
Indianapolis, IN 46206   ages: 2-5

Published by the Children's Better Health Institute for pre-
school level children ages 2-5. Publishes black-and-white or
colored drawings by readers ages 2-5.
Submission Information:
No payment for reader materials. Unused material cannot be
returned. Publisher owns all rights.

U*S*KIDS
1100 Waterway Blvd.
P.O. Box 567
Indianapolis, IN 46206   ages: 5-10

Publication for children from 5-10 from the Children's Better
Health Institute. Stresses health-related themes or ideas

including nutrition, safety, exercise and proper health habits. Publishes from readers; original poetry, original art, Pet Show (a description and photo of favorite pet), and Wacky News (funny stories of not more that 250 words about a U*S*KIDS reader).

Submission Information:
Submissions do not have to be health-related. Please write your name, age, school, complete address, and home phone number on each submission. Material cannot be returned. No payment for published reader material. Sample copies $2.50. Selects material sent by children in the 5-10 age group.

VOICES OF YOUTH ADVOCATES
Scarecrow Press
VOYA Review Editor
4720 Boston Way
Lanham, MD 20708
(Please write for information)

YOUNG VOICES MAGAZINE
P.O. Box 2321
Olympia, WA 98507   grades: K-9

Magazine published bi-monthly. *Young Voices* is by elementary and middle school/junior high students for people interested in their work. Purpose in publishing work by young people: To provide a forum for their creative work.

Submission Information:
Send age, grade and school with submission. Home-schooled writers definitely welcome too. Writer's guidelines available on request. Send SASE. Query first and state subject of your story, essay, or poems. Reports in three weeks. Submit manuscripts and querys to Steve Charak, publisher or Char Simons, editor.

WORD DANCE
Playful Productions, Inc.
59 Pavilions Drive
Manchester, CT 06040   grades: K-8

Magazine published quarterly. A magazine of creative writing
and art that is for and by children in kindergarten through
grade 8. Publishes adventure, fantasy, humor, etc. (fiction);
travel stories and stories based on real-life experiences (nonfiction). Publishes 250 total pieces of writing per year. Length - 3
pages. Publishes Haiku, free verse and other forms of poetry.
Submission Information:
Submit complete manuscripts with submission blanks (submission blank is included in each issue) to Stuart Ungar,
articles editor. Sample copies are available for $4.95. SASE.
Reports in 6-8 months.

THE WRITER'S SLATE
F. Todd Goodson, co-editor
English Department
East Carolina University
Greenville, NC 27858-4353   grades: K-12

Journal published three times per year featuring work from
students in grades K-12. (One issue per contest winner).
Publishes original poetry and prose from students enrolled in
grades K-12.
Submission Information:
Typed manuscripts appreciated, but not necessary. Submission dates are May 15 for fall issue; November 15 for spring
issue.

CONTESTS

PROCEED WITH CAUTION

Contests are an exciting opportunity to enter your work and compete for cash prizes, publishing contracts and other awards. However, before rushing your manuscripts into the mail, take some time and evaluate exactly what you are doing and how much it will cost.

There is always some cost to every submission, from the price of paper and postage, to the fees each contest may require.

We have listed several reputable publishers and sponsors of contests where you may compete without fear of hidden costs or "scams". We do not mean that these are the only legitimate contests available and if you know of other good sponsors, we would appreciate hearing from you.

Some contests try to take advantage of all writers, young and old by promising attractive awards and prizes and then asking you, the author, to pay to have your work published or to collect a prize.

Reputable contests and sponsors don't rely on misleading or false sales tactics so beware of any requests for money (except a legitimate entry fee).

Read all material from the contest carefully and if in doubt, do nothing until you can check with someone who has more experience.

Use the following list as a guideline if you have any questions at all:
- Don't pay for "award" certificates or plaques.
- Don't pay to collect a prize.
- Don't pay "editing" or "reading fees" (if you need help with your manuscript, talk to a local writers group, your teacher, or parents).

Do evaluate the cost of entering a contest by knowing:
- How many contestants will be entering?
- How much are the entry fees?

- What are the awards (certificates, publishing contracts, cash, other prizes, etc?
- Who is the sponsor?
- How are the entry fees to be used?
- Do you have to join the organization or subscribe to something to be entered in the contest?
- Will you be competing with entrants your own age?
- What happens to your rights as the creator?

Know the answers to all these questions **BEFORE** you submit your work and pay the fees.

AIM MAGAZINE'S SHORT STORY CONTEST
P.O. Box 20554
Chicago, IL   grades: High school only

Annual contest sponsored by quarterly publication for high
school, college and general public.
General Information:
No fee to enter. Stories judged by AIM's editorial staff. Deadline is August 15.
Prizes:
First prize-$100; second prize-$50. Winner published in the
autumn issue. We want to show that people from different
ethnic and racial backgrounds are more alike than they are
different. They all strive for the same thing; education, jobs,
good health, etc. Objective is to purge racism from the world
through the written word.

AMHAY MORGAN HORSE LITERARY CONTEST
P.O. Box 960
Shelburne, VT 05482-0960   ages: 22 and under

Sponsored by the American Morgan Horse Association. Open
to all young people under 22.
General Information:
In either essay or poetry form (1,000 words or less), tell in your
own words what the contest theme statement means to you.
Essays and poetry will be judged on general style, originality,
grammar, spelling and punctuation. No entry fee, but you must
attach an official entry form to your poem or essay. Work
submitted may be used for promotional purposes by AMHA.
Participants must be under 22 as of December 1, the contest
deadline. Write the AMHA for current themes and entry form.
Prizes:
Cash awards of $25 will be presented to the winner in both the
essay and poetry categories. Ribbons will be awarded to the
second-through fifth-place winners. Winning entries are published in *The AMHA News & Morgan Sales Network*.

ART RECOGNITION & TALENT SEARCH
National Foundation for Advancement of the Arts
800 Brickell Ave.
Suite 500
Miami, FL 33131   grades: High School Seniors

Annual nonprofit program offers unrestricted cash grants and
scholarship opportunities for high school students gifted in
dance, music, jazz, theater, visual arts, photography and
writing.

General Information:
Contact your teacher, guidance counselor or principal for
complete registration packet. The ARTS program is designed
for high school seniors and other 17-18 year-olds with demon-
strable artistic achievements in dance, music, theater, visual
arts (including film and video) and writing. Application materials sent to individuals upon request. Fee of $25 for each
discipline or discipline category entered by June 1; $35 by
October 1.

Prizes:
Winners receive between $100 and $3,000 in cash. NFAA
earmarks up to $400,000 in cash awards for ARTS applicants
whose works have been judged outstanding by a national panel
of experts. Selected candidates are also invited to Miami, FL
for a week of live adjudications (judging) consisting of : audi-
tions, master and technique classes, workshops, studio exer-
cises and interviews. NFAA pays travel, lodging and meal
expenses for the cash award candidates. Additional college
scholarships and internships worth more than $3 million have
also been made available to all ARTS participants, whether or
not they were award winners. ARTS does not predetermine the
number of awards to be made on any level or in any discipline.
Applicants are judged against a standard of excellence within
each art discipline, not against each other.

BAKER'S PLAYS HIGH SCHOOL
PLAYWRITING CONTEST

Baker's Plays
100 Chauncy St.
Boston, MA 02111   grades: High School Only

Annual contest open to any high school student.

General Information:

Plays should be about "the high school experience," but can also be about any subject, so long as the play can be reasonably produced on the high school stage. Plays may be any length. Multiple submissions or collaorative efforts accepted. Scripts must be accompanied by the signature of a sponsoring high school drama or English teacher, and *it is recommended that the script be given a public stage reading or production prior to the submission.* Teachers may not submit a student's work. The manuscript must be typed and firmly bound, and must come with SASE. Please include enough postage. Plays that do not come with an SASE will not be returned. Do not send originals, copies only. All plays must be postmarked by January 31 each year. Playwrights will be notified in May, send SASE for contest information.

Prizes:

First place receives $500, and the play will be published by Baker's Plays, the September of the contest year. Second place receives $250 and Honorable Mention; third place receives $100 and Honorable Mention. The purpose of the contest is to promote playwriting at the high school level; to promote the production of that work, and to encourage the next generation of playwrights.

BYLINE STUDENT CONTESTS
Student Page Contests
P.O. Box 130596
Edmond, OK 73013   ages: 6-18

Special contests for students during the school year, sponsored by *Byline Magazine,* which is aimed at writers of all ages.
General Information:
Variety of monthly writing contests for students 18 and younger beginning with the September issue and continuing through May each year. All entries must be typed on white bond paper 8-1/2" x11". Put this information in the top left-hand corner of the first page: name, address, city, state,& zip, age and grade, name of school. Have your teacher sign the bottom of the first page, testifying that the entry is your original work. Keep a copy! Entries will not be returned. Please follow the rules, or your entry may be disqualified. Most contests have small entry fees ($1), which provides cash awards to winners. Send SASE for details of upcoming contests. Sample copy $4.00, including postage.
Prizes:
Cash awards and possible publication. Does not publish student work except as winners of writing contests.

CHICKADEE COVER CONTEST
179 John St., Suite 500
Toronto, ON M5T 3G5 Canada   ages: 3-8

Annual contest sponsored in *Chickadee,* a science and nature magazine for children between 3-8, published ten times per year.
General Information:
Create a cover for Chickadee magazine. Use markers, crayons, paints, or make a collage (if you don't use tape) to make your cover. Your cover must be exactly the same size as a real *Chickadee* cover. Leave room at the top for the word *Chickadee.* Don't print the word yourself. Include another piece of paper

with your name, address, age, and postal code. Don't write on your picture. Mail your entry flat with a piece of cardboard. See the Cover Contest announcement for the drawing topic and deadline. It's published in the October issue each year.
Prizes:
The winner is published on the cover of the February issue. Sixteen runners-up are published on pages 2-3.

CRICKET LEAGUE CONTESTS
P.O. Box 300
Peru, IL 61354   ages: All

General Information:
Contest themes vary from month to month. Refer to a current issue of the magazine. Contests are sponsored monthly in one of four categories: Art, Poetry, Short Stories, or Photography. There are two age groups for each contest: 10 and under and 11 and up. All contest rules must be followed . Send SASE to have your work returned. Incomplete entries will not be considered. Rules are listed in each issue. You must have your parent's or guardian's permission to send your entry. Each entry must be signed by your parent or guardian saying it is your own original work and that no one helped you. Deadlines are the 25th of each month.
Prizes:
Winners receive prizes and certificates and most place winners are published in the magazine.

CREATIVE WITH WORDS PUBLICATIONS
Brigitta Geltrich, editor
P.O. Box 223226
Carmel, CA 93922

General Information:
A stamped SASE is a must with all correspondence with CWW. Children must include age or grade attending in school

and a statement of authenticity verified by a responsible adult. Multiple submissions or manuscripts previously published will not be considered for any of the projects. Sample copies are available; Children publications for U.S. $5, Adult and children publications for U.S. $6. Please make check payable to Brigitta Ludgate. Be creative with the English language, research your topic, look at the world from a different perspective, and have fun!

1995 / 1996 Themes: Write for complete details.

1. **We Are Writers, Too! Vol VIII**
   Deadline: June 15, 1995
   (Open to children only - up to 19; responsible adult must verify age of child and authenticity of work)
2. **20 Year Anniversary Contest: "Dreams"**
   Request special guidelines.
3. **Nature Vol III: The Seas; Waters and All Associated With It**
   Deadline: August 31, 1995.
   (Open to adult and children poets and prose writers. Guidelines set by Creative With Words apply)
4. **Nature Vol IV: The Land: Mountains, Continents and All Asscociated With It.**
   Deadline: October 31, 1995
5. **Nature Vol. V: The Forests, the Woods and All Associated With It.**
   Deadline: December 31, 1995
6. **Spooks, Ghosts, Elves, Dwarfs and Such**
   Deadline: January 31, 1996
7. **Dragons, Dinosaurs, Lizards, Crocodiles, Alligators, Snakes and Such**
   Deadline: February 28, 1996
8. **Life's Important Things**
   Deadline: March 31, 1996
   (Open to adult and children poets and prose writers. Guidelines set by CWW apply)
9. **Pets**
   Deadline: April 30, 1996

(Open to adult and children poets and prose writers.
Guidelines set by CWW apply)

10. Nature Vol. VI, The Elements (Air, Fire, Water)
Deadline: May 31, 1996
(Open to adult and children poets and prose writers.
Guidelines set by CWW apply)

THE LOUISE LOUIS/EMILY F. BOURNE
STUDENT POETRY AWARD

Poetry Society of America
15 Gramercy Park
New York, NY 10003   grades: 9-12

Annual contest sponsored by PSA
General Information:
No acknowledgment of receipt of poems, manuscripts, or books
will be made, nor will there be any acknowledgment of incor-
rectly submitted and disqualified submissions. No entries will
be returned. We are unable to accept any corrections or revi-
sions to submissions. Results will announced publicly in late
April. Typed entries must be submitted in duplicate on 8 1/2"
x 11" white paper. The number of lines in the poem and the title
of the contest, including the number of the contest, should be
typed in the upper right corner of the poem submitted, e.g.
Louise Louis/Emily F. Bourne Student Poetry Award (6). Each
submission must be accompanied by a separate cover page
indicating the author's name, address, and telephone numbers. Each cover page should also include the name of the
contest entered, the title of the poem, and the number of lines
and entry fee. All submissions must be sent in one packet
stating member or non-menber on the outside of the envelope.
Multiple pages should be stapled and numbered. Only one
entry may be submitted per contest. Any poem that has
already won a PSA prize may not be resubmitted to another
contest. Submissions must be unpublished on the date of entry
and not scheduled for publication before late April, 1996.
Deadline: Submissions are accepted between October 1 and

December 22. All submissions must be postmarked no later than December 22 if sent first class within the United States. Express Mail or Federal Express packages postmarked after December 22 are not eligible.

Prizes:
This $100 prize is awarded for the best unpublished poem by a high school or preparatory school student (grades 9-12) from the United States. High schools may submit an unlimited number of their students' poems (one submission per student) for $10. There is a $1 entry fee for students submitting single entries (only one entry per student). There is no line limit.

ESSAY CONTEST
The Vegetarian Resource Group
P.O. Box 1463
Baltimore, MD 21203   ages: 18 and under

General Information:
Separate contest categories for students ages 14-18; ages 9-13; and ages 8 and under. Entrants should base their 2-3 page essays on interviewing, research or personal opinion. You do not need to be a vegetarian to enter. Essays can be on any aspect of vegetarianism. All essays become the property of the Vegetarian Resource Group. Each essay needs to include the author's name, age, grade, school, and teacher's name. Entries must be postmarked by May 1 of the contest year. Send SASE for contest guidelines.

Prizes:
A $50 savings bond is awarded in each category. Winning entries are also published in The Vegetarian Journal. Vegetarianism means not eating meat, fish and birds. Among the many reasons for being a vegetarian are beliefs about ethics, culture, health, aesthetics, religion, world peace, economics, world hunger and the environment.

MERLYN'S PEN LITERARY MAGAZINE
CONTEST AND CRITIQUE
P.O. Box 910
East Greenwich, RI 02818   grades: Jr. & Sr. High School

Contest for Intermediate and High School literary magazines, sponsored by Merlyn's Pen; The International Magazines of Student Writing.

General Information:
Separate divisions for high schools and middle schools compete for the Golden Pen Award, honoring the best overall entry. Three optional categories (Best Design, Best Writing, Best Art and Photography) to recognize specific outstanding aspects may also be entered. Judges evaluate the magazines with a comprehensive checklist and a 500-point rating scale. Each entry receives a personalized critique in which an experieinced reviewer evaluates its strengths and weaknesses. Entry forms are included in the last two issues of Merlyn's Pen each school year. Note: Schools do not need to subscribe to enter. Entries need to be postmarked no later than June 30. Winners of awards are notified in mid-September and featured in Merlyn's Pen third issue of the school year. For an entry form and more information, send SASE. Minimum fee $50.

Prizes:
Two recipients of the Golden Pen Award receive recognition in Merlyn's Pen, with pictures of each magazine's staff and advisor, and with selected pages from the magazine. Each of the recipients' schools also earns a Golden Pen trophy. Merlyn's Silver Award (450-500 points) and Merlyn's Bronze Award (400-449 points) also awarded. Winners of the special categories receive plaques. Merlyn's Pen is dedicated to recognizing and publishing the best in student writing and artwork. This contest is designed for school magazines that emphasize creative writing. Our judging includes a detailed critique of art and photography because they so often are a part of literary magazines. But this contest and critique is not appropriate for 'arts' magazines whose main focus is the visual arts.

NATIONAL WRITTEN & ILLUSTRATED BY . . .
AWARDS CONTEST FOR STUDENTS
Landmark Editions,Inc.
1402 Kansas Ave.
Kansas City, MO 64127   ages: 6-19

Annual book contest for students.
General Information:
Original books may be entered in one of three age categories:
6-9, 10-13 and 14-19. Each book must be written and illustrated by the same student. Entry must be signed by parent/
guardian and teacher. Home-schooled students may enter, but
entry must be signed by a librarian or teacher other than a
parent/guardian. Send a #10 SASE with $.64 postage for
complete rules and guidelines.
Prizes:
Winners receive all-expense-paid trips to Landmark's offices
in Kansas City, where editors and art directors assist them in
preparing their text and illustrations for the publication of
their books. Winners also receive publishing contracts and are
paid royalties.

PUBLISH-A-BOOK CONTEST &
YOUNG PUBLISH-A-BOOK CONTEST
Raintree/Steck-Vaughn Publishers
P.O. Box 27010
Austin, TX 78755
(800) 531-5015

Publish-a-Book Contest for grades 4-6
Young Publish-a-Book Contest for grades 2-3
General Information:
New contest theme announced each fall. The Publish-a-Book
Contest is open to all students in grades 2-6 enrolled in
accredited public or private schools in the United States, all
U.S. territories, and Canada. Stories on the theme of "Myster-
ies" may be fiction or nonfiction, but they must be orginal. Each

entry must be submitted by a sponsor, who must be a teacher or librarian at the school the student attends or a local public librarian. Each entry must be written by a student who is in grades 2-6 during the 1995-96 school year. Each entry may have only one author, and each author may submit only one entry. Illustrated manuscripts will not be accepted, as the winning stories will be professionally illustrated. Entries for grades 2-3 should be between 300 and 500 words, and entries for grades 4-6 should be between 700 and 900 words in length. All entries should be typed, double-spaced. The student must put his or her name, home address and telephone number on the first page only of the entry. A separate top cover sheet must contain the following information: the student's name, home address and telephone number with area code; the student's current grade level; the sponsor's name; and the name, address and telephone number of the sponsor's school or library. Entries must be postmarked by January 31, 1996. Winners will be selected by May 1, 1996. Winners and sponsors will be notified thereafter by phone or mail. All entries become the property of Raintree/Steck-Vaughn Publishers and cannot be returned. Previous winners are not eligible to participate.

Prizes:

Raintree/Steck-Vaughn will publish the Grand Prize entries in January, 1997. Each Grand Prize Winner will receive a $500 advance against an author royalty contract, as well as 10 copies of the published book. The sponsor or each of the winning entries will receive 20 free books from the Raintree/Steck-Vaughn catalog. Each Honorable Mention Winner will receive $25, and their sponsors will receive 10 free books from the catalog.

REFLECTIONS SCHOLARSHIP COMPETITION
The National PTA
330 North Wabash Ave., Suite 2100
Chicago, IL 60611-3690

The Reflections Scholarship Competition is directed toward

students who wish to pursue the arts in their future education.
General Information:
Each student must be a senior in high school; participate in the
1995-96 Reflections Program through his/her local PTA or
PTSA; submit two (2) original works; submit a completed
application packet. The deadline for requesting an application
is the last Friday in November. After that date, applications
may be requested from your local PTA office. All requests must
include the national ID number for your local PTA unit which
can be acquired through your local unit president or state
office. Winners are announced in March.
Prizes:
The Reflections Scholarship Competition consists of four scholarships of $750 each, one in each of four art areas: Literature,
music, photography and visual arts.

REFLECTIONS CULTURAL ARTS PROGRAM
The National PTA
330 North Wabash Avenue, Suite 2100
Chicago, IL 60611-3690

The Reflections Cultural Arts Program was designed to provide opportunities for students in pre-school through the
twelfth grade to express and share their creative abilities.
Each year works of art are inspired by a theme which is chosen
from hundreds of student theme entries.
General Information:
Each entry must be the work of one student. Each student and
his/her parent or guardian must sign the affirmation sentence
on the Official Entry Form stating that the entry is original.
Art work may be created in or outside of school. Categories of
participation include: Literature (Pre-school-2nd grade); Music (Intermediate 3-5th grades); Photography (Middle/Junior
6-8th grades); Visual Arts (Senior 9-12th grades).

Only the state PTA's may submit entries to the National
Level. The National PTA awards first, second and third place
in each arts area, in each grade division. Honorable mentions

may be chosen in each art category and grade division. One outstanding Interpretation winner is chosen from the place winners in each arts area (total of four). State presidents will receive a list of the winners in May. Students receive a letter of congratulations or regret. All participants receive a certificate. Deadlines are set by each local PTA. Any questions regarding deadlines or rules should be directed to the state PTA.

Prizes:

PTA awards first, second and third place in each arts category and grade division. Winners receive $300, $200 or $100, a certificate and a book is donated to each of their schools. The Outstanding Interpretation winners receive an expense-paid trip to the National PTA convention with one adult, a $250 scholarship and a gold plated Reflections Medallion.

TEEN POWER POETRY CONTEST
Box 632
Glen Ellyn, IL 60138   ages: 12-16

General Information:

An annual contest for ages 12-16 which is announced in August. Deadline is first Friday in January. Entries must have a Christian, spiritual emphasis. Include name, address, age, and hobbies with entry. Entry cannot be returned.

TEEN POWER TRUE STORY CONTEST
Box 632
Glen Ellyn, IL 60138   ages: 12-16

General Information:

Annual contest announced in January for ages 12-16. Deadline is May 31 each year. Stories should be 600-1000 words and must have spiritual emphasis: how God has worked in the life of the author or someone he or she knows. Send name, address, age, and hobbies with entry. Winners are notified by mail and stories are printed in the September issue. Entries cannot be

returned.
Prizes:
First place: $100
Second place: 75
Third place: 50

WRITING CONTESTS
The Writing Conference, Inc.
P.O. Box 664
Ottawa, KS 66067   grades: 3-12

Contests sponsored by The Writing Conference, a nonprofit
organization that provides services to any children, young
adults and teachers interested in reading and writing.
General Information:
Students in grades 3-12 are invited to submit poetry, narration
or exposition on selected topics each year. Send SASE in
August for yearly topics and guidelines. Deadline in January.
Prizes:
Winners in each category receive plaques. In addition, winning
entries are published in *The Writer's Slate*. First-place winners, their parents and their teachers are guests at the Satur-
day luncheon of the Annual Conference on Writing and Literature held every spring in Kansas City.

MANUSCRIPT LOG

Title of Book _____

Date Mailed _____

Mr/Mrs. _____
(Name of Editor)

Address _____

City _____ State ___ Zip _____

Phone # _____

Response Date _____

MANUSCRIPT LOG

Title of Book _____

Date Mailed _____

Mr/Mrs. _____
(Name of Editor)

Address _____

City _____ State ___ Zip _____

Phone # _____

Response Date _____

MANUSCRIPT LOG

Title of Book _____

Date Mailed _____

Mr/Mrs. _____
(Name of Editor)

Address _____

City _____ State ___ Zip _____

Phone # _____

Response Date _____

MANUSCRIPT LOG

Title of Book _____
Date Mailed _____
Mr/Mrs. _____
                    (Name of Editor)

Address _____
City _____ State ___ Zip _____
Phone # _____
Response Date _____

MANUSCRIPT LOG

Title of Book _____
Date Mailed _____
Mr/Mrs. _____
                    (Name of Editor)

Address _____
City _____ State ___ Zip _____
Phone # _____
Response Date _____

MANUSCRIPT LOG

Title of Book _____
Date Mailed _____
Mr/Mrs. _____
                    (Name of Editor)

Address _____
City _____ State ___ Zip _____
Phone # _____
Response Date _____

Glossary

Advance. The amount of money paid to an author up front, before publication, that will be deducted from the future royalties.

All rights. The rights that permit the publisher to use the work in any form without additional royalties or payments to the author or artist.

Contract. A legal agreement that specifies the rights purchased by the publisher and the amount of payment the author or artist will receive for that sale.

Copyright. A legal right that protects the author's or artist's work from being copied or used by someone else without payment.

Cover letter. A letter accompanying a manuscript or book proposal.

Credit list. A list of published works.

Feedback. The reaction of other people to your work.

Fiction. A general term for an imaginative work, usually prose. Novels and short stories are fiction.

Format. The form in which the publisher wants to see work submitted. There are some standard forms for manuscripts, but some publishers may have specific requirements.

Genre. A kind of literary work, such as poetry, romance, historical fiction, etc.

IRC. International Redemption Coupon. IRC's are issued by the postal service and should accompany submissions to foreign countries that require a SASE. Contact your local post office for more information.

One-Time Rights. The publisher's right to publish an article or story in a magazine or book form one time only. The rights then return to the author, and the author may resell the same article somewhere else. One-time rights are more likely to be granted by magazines than book publishers.

Proofreading. Reading a manuscript carefully to correct spelling, grammar, punctuation, and typographical errors.

Query. A letter written to an editor by an author describing an idea for a story or an article.

Rejection Slip. A note from a publisher that tells you your work has not been accepted.

Revise. Rewriting, reworking, and polishing a story or manuscript.

Royalties. A percentage of sales paid to the author based on the retail price of the book.

SASE. Abbreviation for Self-Addressed Stamped Envelope. Most publishers will not return your manuscript to you without one.

Self-publishing. Publishing that is supported financially by the author.

Submit. Sending a manuscript off to a publisher. That manuscript is often called a "submission."

Writer's Group. A group of writers who meet together to critique their work, share market tips, and celebrate successes.

Writer's Guidelines. A description prepared by a publisher that describes their current publishing needs.

RECOMMENDED READING

*How to Write a Children's Book
and get it published*
Barbara Seuling
Charles Scribner's Sons

*A Writer's Guide to a
Children's Book Contract*
Mary Flower
Fern Hill Books

*Children's Writer's and
Illustrator's Market*
Christine Martin
Writers Digest Books

Market Guide for Young Writers
Kathy Henderson
Writers Digest Books

For more information about books written by children:

Raspberry Publications
POB 925
Westerville, OH 43086-6925
1.800.759.7171
Fax 1.614.899.6147